Completing The Course

Completing The Course

A Fairy Tale
Set in the School of Life

Tom Nussbaum

On Course Books • Seattle, Washington

ON COURSE BOOKS
P.O. Box 20687
Seattle, WA 98102

Library of Congress Catalog Card Number:
97-92585

ISBN 0-9660115-0-3

Printed in the United States of America

First printing 1997

Photography: Tracy Lamb
Cover design: Laughing Lamb Design, Seattle, WA

Acknowledgments

Many people deserve thanks for their contributions to *Completing The Course*. This is my first novel, and each person helped me fulfill a lifelong dream with their assistance, patience, encouragement, or inspiration.

Ray Woods recognized, many years ago, my need to create, and while he did not live to see my dream become reality, his spirit hovered over me, guiding me throughout the entire process of creating this book. I often felt him over my shoulder, reading the work-in-progress and whispering words and ideas into my ear that greatly improved the story.

Annie and Mar, Jay, Kurt, Christine, Randy, Jeff, Gloria, Barbara, Moira, and Jonathan each contributed to *Completing The Course* by reading early drafts, and their comments and suggestions were both helpful and greatly appreciated.

Brian and Sue helped me understand computers in the early stages of this project. But it was John Higinbotham who became my computer guru. John literally saved this novel, and my sanity, with his knowledge and assistance, never complaining about my computer illiteracy, constant state of panic, and countless requests.

I appreciate that my sister and father, who read early drafts of the book, have neither disowned me nor scheduled me on one of those embarrassing-relative episodes on talk TV. Instead, they have encouraged me to follow my dream. I also appreciate that my mother, who was not allowed to read *Completing The Course* prior to publication, waited patiently, without grumbling.

Special thanks go to my production team headed by Thatcher, Cathy, and Tracy. Their help and experience have been invaluable.

And I must thank the two dynamic young men who are responsible for my writing this particular story. First, I acknowledge J, who, unknowingly, said the words that triggered this novel with an innocent comment that activated my curiosity, creativity, and imagination.

Finally, I thank D who inspired me to complete this course. Without him, this book would never have been written. He courageously allowed me to enter his life, examine his soul, and, then, twist what I found into fiction. He is my inspiration, my mentor, my friend. He is my Shepherd. He is why I learned the importance of *Completing The Course*. —TN

course (kors) n. 1: progress, passage; also, direction of progress 2: the ground or path over which something moves 3: the part of a meal served at one time 4: an ordered series of acts or proceedings: sequence of events 5: method of procedure: conduct, behavior 6: a series of instruction periods dealing with a subject 7: the series of studies leading to graduation from a school or college 8: *Naut.* a point on the compass, esp. the one toward which one is sailing

PROLOGUE

It was a pretty typical teenage boy's bedroom for the 1960s. Posters of the New York Jets, Green Bay Packers, and Notre Dame Fighting Irish covered one wall. The Rolling Stones stared menacingly at them from the wall across the room, Mick Jagger's leering lips daring anyone to object. Several hand-painted model sports-cars idled on a dusty pine dresser. A desk covered with doodle-decorated Pee-Chee folders sat, ignored, in the corner, two small sports trophies resting at the back.

A maze of dirty clothes on the floor blocked access to the closet. Its door stood ajar, exposing an empty white wicker hamper with its lid raised. The room's window and blinds were closed, trapping a stifling, stale male odor in the squalid space. A tiny light on the nightstand tried unsuccessfully to illuminate the bedroom's dim grayness. The bed was unmade; one corner of the wrinkled white bottom sheet had crept up, exposing the stained mattress.

From a record player balanced on a wooden crate under the window, Mick and the other Stones roared at a volume that announced to the neighbors that no adults, no parents, were in the house. They had gone away for the weekend to escape the mid-summer heat.

Two teenage boys lounged on the disheveled bed in the near darkness of the room. Three empty beer bottles lay next to the smaller lad. A fourth was in his hand. His bleary eyes and awkward movements made evident the effects of several beers on a slightly built, empty-

stomached teenager on a sweaty summer night. A nearly full beer bottle balanced next to the other youth. He intended to stay sober. He
had to, he felt, to clearly experience what was about to happen. It
was his room.

"Hey, hurry up and finish that," ordered the bigger boy.

"OK. But you've barely finished off one, Man. I'm way ahead of
you," slurred the other.

"Don't worry about me!" snapped the youth defensively. Then
his tone changed, immediately becoming cheerful, artificially cheerful, to hide his thoughts. "Hey, wanna wrestle?"

Before the lad had a chance to respond, the bigger boy leaped
unexpectedly from the bed to the floor and grabbed the boy's right
arm, sending his beer bottle across the bed, its contents spilling on
the twisted sheets.

"Let go, Man! I don't want to wrestle."

"Wanna get fucked then?" the teenager asked without warning, as
he wrenched the boy's spindly arm into a tight behind-the-back ham-
merlock, lifting him forcefully to his feet. It was more a threat than a
question.

"Ow!" yelped the boy as he ineffectively struggled to escape.
"What the hell are you doing?"

"I'm gonna fuck your ass, you little pansy. You want to be part of
my crowd, hang with me and my friends, don't you? Huh? Just how
far will you go, Man, to be one of the 'cool' guys?"

"This isn't funny. Let go," the trapped prisoner whined.

"No. It isn't funny. It's fun! For me! Now drop your pants, or I'll
do it for you."

The boy was startled with disbelief. It had never dawned on him
that rape would be a part of this evening, that rape would be the price
he would have to pay to be accepted by the bigger boy and his
friends. Though his thought process was slowed by the alcohol, he
realized he was hopelessly overpowered. He would not be able to
escape. He would have to submit. He was smaller, weaker, and he was
drunk. No one could say he just let it happen. Or that he wanted it
to happen. In an illogical situation, that was the only logic he could
find. Resigned to the inevitable, he lowered his pants and white briefs
with his free hand.

"That's a good little queer," chided his assailant. "Now bend over."

As the humiliated youth bent forward, urged by a painful upward yank on his arm, he heard spitting noises and felt something wet and firm touch him. His entire body tightened.

He looked up to see himself in the dresser-mounted mirror across the room, staring back in pain. And he could see in the reflection, hovering over his shoulder, the gleaming, glazed eyes of the madman who was viciously, violently violating him.

In the background, Mick Jagger disdainfully sang *It's All Over Now*.

• ⇀

Some people make no impression when you first meet them. You forget their name as they are saying it. Others make a bad impression—bad posture, bad breath, bad attitude, or whatever. But then there are those you like immediately, mysteriously connecting with them, subtly welcoming them into your world and silently giving them permission to stay. Steven Shepherd was one of those people.

But before I tell you about Steven and how we met, let me tell you who I am. My name is Tim Lerner. I'm forty-two years old, look about thirty, often feel about seventy, and sometimes think and act like twenty. I'm a speech therapist at a Portland, Oregon, high school.

I became a speech therapist because, as a young child, I had a severe lisp, which was corrected by a miracle-working angel appropriately named Miss Sayer. As soon as Miss Sayer began working her magic on me, teaching me how to eliminate the sibilance from my speech, I knew that I, too, wanted to positively affect other people's communication. I also knew that I loved Miss Sayer. She was my first schoolboy crush.

Unlike Miss Sayer, who focused on early childhood speech impediments, I primarily work with newly arrived immigrants from Southeast Asia, Africa, and Latin America, trying to improve their English pronunciation. Because I work with the relatively small group of English-as-a-second-language students, I have little opportunity to meet the other pupils at my school. Therefore, meeting Steven Shepherd was an unusual event, one that would have an immense impact on both our lives.

I came to Columbia High nearly five years ago in September of 1989, reporting at 7:30 in the morning on staff preparation day. I was met at the door by a petite woman with a close-cropped Afro.

"New faculty and staff are to meet in the conference room next to the library. Go to the second floor," she ordered with authority, blocking the doorway.

"What is this?" I asked, unintimidated. "Freshman hazing?"

"Exactly," she answered coldly. But her smiling eyes betrayed her.

"Are pledge paddles involved?" I played along.

"We're Cougars here. We use cat-o'-nine-tails!" she teased. "The stairs are right there," she directed, pointing to the route to the second floor.

The conference room was filled with nearly a dozen people anxiously, awkwardly, excitedly making introductions and small talk. I joined them, quickly filling out a name tag and filling up a paper cup with coffee. Moments later, the woman who had just mock-bullied me in front of the office entered the room. The smile in her eyes had spread to her mouth.

"I'm Palla McGuire. How is everybody?" she said enthusiastically. "The faculty is waiting in the library to meet all of you."

"Please, finish your coffee in here because as each of your names is called, you are to run—yes, run—into the library, where a rally girl will toss a pompom to each of the women and a student body officer will throw a football to each of the guys. I know, it sounds sexist, dated, and corny, but it is a long-standing school tradition. Besides it will start the meeting in a positive, energetic mood," Palla assured us, as skepticism spread across each new faculty member's face.

After several names were called, mine was announced, and I reluctantly ran into the bright, skylight-lit library. A tall, handsome young man fired a football toward me. The throw was strong and direct, but not hard. It reached its target perfectly. I did not drop the ball. And through that symbolic act, I first became aware of Steven Shepherd.

The final new teacher, a young blonde woman with a short, boyish haircut, followed me. She caught her pompom and joined the rest of us at a table marked with a "Welcome Cougar Cubs" sign as the cheering and applause ended. The young man who had rifled the football to me stood facing the crowd and spoke.

"Welcome to Columbia High. You are Cougars now!" he greeted us. And welcome back to the rest of the faculty and staff. For those of you who don't know me, I'm Steven Shepherd and I'm ASB president," he said in a clear confident voice. Then he introduced the other officers: shy Sherri Hunter, tiny Tina Perez, and Brett Weiss, wearing a torn, black Guns N' Roses T-shirt. The rally squad was introduced next, and they performed a short, shrill yell, most of which I could not understand.

"Now, Ladies and Gentlemen," Steven boomed in a theatrical delivery, "the man who heads Columbia High; the man, who it seems, gives his entire life to us and this school; the man who makes Columbia a 'grim' place, our principal, Mr. Gregory Grimm."

The sounds of clapping, whistling, and laughter filled the air as Steven sat down next to Brett, and a fiftyish, pepper-haired man with determination in his eyes rose to speak.

As Mr. Grimm talked about the coming school year, Steven appeared to whisper something to Brett, a smaller, more boyish, less athletic-looking lad. Then both boys smiled slightly, perhaps sharing a private joke or observation, and I realized that Steven's piercing eyes were directed at me. I looked away quickly, refocusing on the principal's words as he released us to set up our classrooms or offices for the year.

After the welcoming ceremony, I rushed out to unload the boxes of books, files, and papers that were crammed in my trunk and stacked on the back seat of my car. It took ten trips, and half an hour, to unload completely.

But I could not unload the vision of Steven's quizzical smile or his penetrating eyes. What had he said to Brett? I wondered. Were they planning a schoolboy prank on me, the new guy? Or were they merely assessing all the new staff members with typical teenage judgments like "geek," "babe," "lame old dinosaur," and "cool dude"?

I next saw Steven at the first assembly of the year the following Friday. Again demonstrating his dynamic personality, he welcomed the students, especially the freshmen and transfers, to Columbia and, with great poise and charm, explained the direction in which he intended to lead the student body. Then participants in fall sports were introduced by Mr. Grimm, culminating in the introduction of the football team by Coach Sam Martinson. The rally squad showed their school spirit and urged others to show theirs by attending the season-opening football game that night.

And I did. I don't know why. I had no obligation to go. I didn't know any of the players. I really didn't feel a part of the school yet. I don't even enjoy high school athletics that much. And I had other things to do. But I went.

I sat by myself high up in the stands, above most of the students, among the other faculty, parents, and alumni. I spent the first half of the game watching the spectacle around me: the activity, the rally girls, the people, the deepening darkness of the sky, and, oh yes, the game. And then, sooner than I expected, with a startling blast from an irritating horn, the first half of the game was over, with the Cougars leading 10–7.

Almost immediately, I noticed Steven climbing the stairs toward me, smiling.

"I saw you sitting up here," he said as he neared me. "Thanks for coming to the game. Usually new teachers don't get involved for a while. By the way, I'm Steven Shepherd, in case you don't remember me," he offered, introducing himself officially.

"Mr. Lerner," I said, returning the formality with a cautious handshake. "I'm the new speech therapist and, having heard you speak a few times now, I'll bet that you'll never have to come to my office."

"Well, probably not," Steven conceded with a laugh. "But you never know. Listen," he added, looking toward the first rows of student seats, "I've got to get back to my friends down there. It was nice meeting you. I'm sure we'll run into each other again."

• ⟶

Steven and I did run into each other again less than a week later. Actually, we didn't run into each other. It was planned. By Steven.

The final bell of the day had just rung. I was having a face-off with my computer. It wasn't listening to me, and I, apparently, did not understand what it was saying.

"Dammit," I mumbled under my breath. "I'm the smart one here. This nationality code is correct," I insisted. The computer stared at me in silent defiance as students and faculty scurried past my open door. Bits of conversation followed them like balloons tied to their belt loops. Metallic locker noises echoed off the hallway walls. Outside my window, in the parking lot, a succession of engines ignited, horns honked, and tires talked in screeching tones.

A light knock on my door interrupted the end-of-day symphony. I looked up. There stood Steven, royal blue backpack hanging on his left shoulder. He was wearing beige slacks and a button-down-collar, white dress shirt. It was then that I realized that Steven, while only seventeen, easily looked twenty. His older physical appearance complemented his naturally mature manner. I realized, too, that I had never seen him in jeans, shorts, a T-shirt, or Nikes, the costume of conformity worn by most of his peers.

"Excuse me, Mr. Lerner, but do you have a minute? There's something I'd like to ask you," Steven asked quietly, almost timidly.

"Go for it!" I responded, intrigued.

"Would it be OK if I interviewed you for my writing skills class? You see, we're supposed to interview someone here at school we don't know very well. I think Ms. Mueller really wants us to meet a student we don't usually talk to. But I'd love to interview you, find out more about you, like why you chose speech therapy as a career and where you went to school. Stuff like that," Steven jabbered rapidly without taking a breath.

"Oh, that's cool, I guess," I sputtered, quite surprised. "Do you want to do the interview now?"

"Well, sure, if it's convenient," he answered as I closed the folder on my desk, allowing him to take a tablet out of his backpack and a black felt-tip pen from his shirt pocket. "Geeze, where to start?"

For more than half an hour the young writer asked me about my life, schooling, career, and hobbies. I talked freely, answering honestly the questions he posed, all the while wondering why the interest in my life.

"What do you like best about your job?" he asked as the interview wound down.

"Well, that's easy. The students. I like working with you guys the best. But as the school speech therapist, I'm this mystery person that few of the students get to know," I told Steven. "I don't work with most of you. I don't have you in class. I don't give grades or fail people. I'm a nonthreatening, neutral adult here. Therefore, I can become a nonjudgmental ear or shoulder for kids who need someone to talk to. I really enjoy serving in that role when it comes up. And sometimes having a neutral adult around to bounce ideas and feelings off is a pretty good thing. I think I've helped former students get through some tough times. Maybe I can do that here, too."

I really had not aimed this message directly at Steven. He appeared to have his life in control, to exude confidence, and to possess a strong sense of self. There were other kids out there, I thought, who could better use my "nonjudgmental ear or shoulder," kids whose lives were in more disarray than Steven's seemed to be. Perhaps he could take the message to them.

"Thank you. This has been really interesting," Steven said, concluding his questions with a thoughtful tone in his voice. He stood, put his pen back into his pocket, and massaged his right wrist. "Whew, that was a lot of writing, Mr. Lerner. But you know what? I'm glad I interviewed you. You're pretty cool," he flattered as he swung his backpack over his left shoulder. "For a teacher." And he was gone.

•➤

As I left school following Steven's departure, I stopped in the main office to check my mailbox. A mysterious surprise awaited me there, a surprise that both puzzled and frightened me greatly. Nestled in my mailbox, under a union newsletter and an updated computer printout of students receiving speech therapy, was a pink piece of paper cut into a triangle. "Thanks for being here" was typed in bold-face across it. There was no signature.

What the hell, I thought as I picked it up, pushing it into my jacket pocket before anyone could see it. Who is this from? What does it mean? I questioned, trying to decipher its ambiguity. Is it a note of appreciation from the administration?

Could it be as innocent as that? Could it be merely a coincidence that a pink triangle was used as a thank-you note? Or had the pink triangle been used intentionally by someone who had seen my car and recognized the small, scraped, faded decal decorating the rear bumper? The pink triangle! The pink triangle that says "never again" to persecution like that inflicted on countless homosexuals by Nazis during the Holocaust. The pink triangle I defiantly displayed knowing that, less than a year before, voters had overturned the governor's order protecting state employees, like public school teachers, from discrimination based on sexual orientation.

But that was the extent to which I demonstrated my defiance, because I never discussed my personal life or political views with my co-workers. I never socialized with them. I completely separated my life from theirs. Except for a worn, pale pink decal, professionally, I hid in the closet. I worked, after all, in a school. In Oregon.

Is another lesbian or gay teacher simply announcing in a cautious manner his or her presence? I wondered. Or did this come from a student? And, if so, which one? And under what circumstances? Was this a sincere note from a student struggling with sexual orientation issues? Or was I on the verge of being harassed, even blackmailed?

All these questions and more raced through my mind in the short, claustrophobic moment I stood in front of my mailbox. I slammed the box shut and, dodging everyone between the office and the main door, escaped into the freeing fresh air.

But I was not free of the feeling that I was being watched by hidden eyes, eyes that I could not see, eyes that, perhaps, were not even there. I raced to my car as quickly as I had ever done at the end of a school day. But what the rush was, I was not certain, for when I settled myself behind the steering wheel, I just sat there, staring at the pink triangle note, reflecting on its significance and its possible source.

As I turned the key in the ignition, my thoughts were shattered by the lyrics of a Sixties Buffalo Springfield song on the radio—"Paranoia strikes deep. Into your life it will creep." The words taunted me, and I realized that the answers to all my questions would not come to me sitting there in the parking lot. I would have to ask other staff if they had received notes of appreciation from the administration. If they had not, I simply would have to wait for the sender to act again or reveal himself.

As I drove home, my mind shifted back to thoughts of Steven's interview. Had I said the right thing? Was my message clear? Would Steven pass it on to others? Or would he somehow misinterpret my words?

• ➤

Apparently, Steven did interpret my message correctly, because several days later, he appeared at my door again.

"Hi. How are things going?" he asked.

"Fine," I responded. "And to what do I owe this surprise visit?"

"I wanted to let you know that I got an 'A' on the interview."

"Well, of course you did," I smiled. "You had the perfect subject."

"Yeah, that's it," Steven agreed, playing along with the joke. "But I also came here to ask you something I'm curious about. It's kind of personal, so you don't have to answer if you don't want to," he said, teasing my imaginative mind.

"Ask, and we'll see, Steven," I urged suspiciously.

"Mr. Lerner, what do you think of Barry Goldwater?" the young man asked directly.

"Barry Goldwater? The senator that ran for president back in the Sixties?" I replied, visibly surprised. "Well, even though I was pretty young back then, I know I didn't like him. Dad said he was sort of crazy, a reactionary, radical conservative Republican. Today, though, I look at him quite differently. I actually respect him. He's been a pretty honest politician, which is a contradiction in itself, I suppose. He's distanced himself from current conservatives. He's actually reasonably moderate by today's standards. But, why, Steven, of all the things you might have asked me, are you interested in my opinion of Barry Goldwater?" I questioned with a little laugh.

"Dad worked on Goldwater's '64 campaign when he was a teenager. So I grew up knowing about him. I was just curious," he explained. "Thanks for not blowing off my question, Mr. Lerner. Got to go," he added as he stepped out the door and down the hall, leaving me staring after him, amused and confused.

• ✦

My confusion was eased somewhat when the first edition of the school newspaper, *The Chronicle,* was delivered later that day. "Just Do It . . . All, Apparent Shepherd Motto" blared the banner headline across page one. Below the headline was a photograph of Steven standing in front of the school's main door. Quickly, I began to scan the article about the student body president, knowing it was meant to introduce him to the new students at Columbia and let the other students learn more about him. But I also hoped the story would give me some insights into who Steven Shepherd was, what made him tick, and why he seemed drawn to me. Or was I just imagining that he seemed drawn to me?

The lengthy article painted a picture of Steven that both did and did not surprise me. I had realized immediately upon seeing Steven that he was a dynamic young man. I didn't realize how dynamic.

According to the article, Steven had been both freshman and junior class president. He was captain of the track team and a state champion miler. He rarely wore his letterman jacket, though, because he didn't "feel he was any better than those students without jackets. Besides," Steven explained, "running is not who I am. It is just something I do."

Apparently, it was something he did exceptionally well, because several important college track coaches and former Olympics competitors had been following his career and were showing interest in his future.

Steven also had been an important part of the drama department during his sophomore and junior years, enjoying lead and supporting roles equally. He also played the accordion.

A devout Catholic and a regular church-goer, Steven volunteered to watch preschoolers during services and meetings. He also sang with the church's youth choir, which often visited senior centers, homeless shelters, and group homes for the disabled.

Scholastically, his grades would have qualified him for any college or university, let alone the in-state schools, had he applied. But he had not.

Steven's postgraduate plans were to join the army.

"Everyone, I think, should serve their country in some way," the student leader expounded. "I wish we had some kind of military and/or social service draft. Then every eighteen-year-old would have to choose some military branch or civilian service to join. I've chosen two-year duty with the army, partially out of patriotism, partially because I think it will make me a stronger person, and partially because of the economic and scholastic benefits," he continued. "College, and perhaps running, will come later."

I read this part again. The army? Steven's going into the army, I said to myself in disbelief. I read his plan, his explanation, a third time, hoping it was an hallucination.

The reporter's final request of the contemplative young Mr. Shepherd had been that he describe himself. "Wow," Steven had responded, "I think I'm just a God-fearing Catholic guy who tries his hardest at whatever he does, who cares about people, who tries to make a difference in the world around him, and who wants to 'do the right thing,' as Spike Lee might say." He tagged on, "I guess I'm an old-time Goldwater Republican, too."

I looked up, my jaw slack. My God, I thought, this is one helluva kid. He's beyond interesting. He's entered the realm of intriguing. And why would he have asked my impression of Barry Goldwater if he had already formed his own opinion? Why would my view even matter?

For several minutes, I stared straight ahead, wondering what more I would learn about Steven Shepherd and beginning to understand why he fascinated me as he did. Then, realizing the time, I picked up *The Chronicle* and my jacket and headed for home. Thank God it was Friday!

•⇀

Later that evening, as I ate my Cheap Chef chicken fricassee dinner, I read the article again. This time, however, something connected in my head. Had I been blind? Steven Shepherd is "the best little boy in the world." *I* had been "the best little boy in the world." Through the years, several gay friends had also described themselves as having been "the best little boy in the world." There was even a book called *The Best Little Boy in the World* about growing up gay.

Every "best little boy," it seemed, overachieved, overcompensated, kept out of trouble, and was good, kind, and admirable for one reason: They wanted people to like them. If they were liked, then one flaw would not make a difference. But they hid that flaw, a flaw for which they felt extremely guilty, embarrassed, and ashamed. They hid that flaw because they dreadfully feared it would cost them their family, friends, and, perhaps, their life. And they hid that flaw, that alleged flaw, even though they desperately wanted, needed, to share it with those for whom they cared.

Oh my, I gasped under my breath. Could Steven Shepherd be gay? Is that what all this is about? Did he leave the mystifying note in my mailbox? No. Wait. I'm jumping to conclusions. He has not given me any real reasons to believe that he is gay. My imagination is working overtime. Maybe this is wishful thinking—besides, if he had seen the pink triangle on my car, why would he even know what it symbolizes? *Put this out of your mind. Now!* I ordered myself as I tossed the Cheap Chef carton into the garbage. Frankly, I thought, I should have tossed it there before I ate its contents.

Unbelievably, I was able to put Steven out of my mind. I succeeded in stifling any questions about him and any assumptions or thoughts I had regarding our growing relationship. Until Monday morning, that is.

• ⤳

I had just unlocked the door and entered my office when Steven appeared, from nowhere. His backpack, still straddling his shoulders, indicated he had not yet been to his locker. Urgency was splashed across his face like the sting of early morning after-shave.

"Hi," he greeted me, with concern in his voice. "Did you read the article on me in Friday's paper?"

"Of course I did," I responded. "I learned a lot about you. You are one busy guy. A busy guy with a plan."

"Yeah, I guess I am. But did I sound arrogant in that article?" he asked, side-stepping my comment. "I've read it over and over this week-end, and I think it made me appear too perfect. I sounded like a know-it-all giving a lecture." Then Steven paused, looked me in the eyes, and said apologetically, "I'm not that good, Mr. Lerner. I'm no saint."

Sensing Steven's serious tone, I searched for an appropriate sup-portive comment. "Well, first of all, I don't think you sounded arro-gant. You sounded mature, responsible and . . . deep." I visibly cringed when I heard myself say "deep." It sounded so Sixties. Steven flickered a smile. "But is that what's really bothering you?" Steven's smile faded. "Are you kicking yourself because you sounded too good to be true or because you think you're not as good as you should be? Either way, please stop. You're great just the way you are!" I paused and released a little ironic laugh. "Now that's what a lecture sounds like," I concluded.

Attempting to lighten the conversation, I casually asked, "Other than that, how was your weekend?"

"OK, I guess. No. Actually it really sucked," he corrected himself. "I went to the game Friday night with Brett, and I asked him what he thought of the article. He's the one who said I sounded arrogant. Then we started arguing about a lot of stuff, and he started in again on the army thing, which he just doesn't understand, and I said some things I shouldn't have said, that I don't even mean. And tons of peo-ple were listening. I mean it was right there in the stands." Steven took a deep breath. "He left at half-time, and we haven't talked since. I've really felt like crap all weekend."

"Whoa, Steven. There's a lot going on here. But first I'm confused about a key piece of information. Who is Brett?" I asked, puzzled.

"Brett Weiss, the ASB treasurer," responded the troubled teenager, a bit irritated. "I thought you'd met him. Anyway he's been my best friend since the first day of kindergarten. But there are things about me he just doesn't understand, can't understand, like my wanting to join the army. On the other hand, I don't really get his obsession with black clothes and heavy metal bands. And don't even get me started on his taste in girls. Weirdoes. All of them. Really strange," he criticized. "He could do so much better. Oh, that really sounds judgmental, doesn't it? Anyway, it's his business. We are best friends, though. We've gone through a lot together."

Although I had seen Brett occasionally since school had started, I'd never seen him with Steven. I had no reason to believe their friendship went beyond their ASB positions. Judging by their appearances, too, their close friendship came as a surprise. After all, Steven's style was that of a preppie. Brett, shorter and pudgier, wore tattered jeans and dirty black T-shirts promoting bands that allegedly urge their fans to kill household pets, farm animals, and even themselves.

"Good friends are a rare quantity," I said quietly, searching for the right words for Steven's situation. "They should be allowed to express their feelings without worrying about repercussions. Maybe he didn't really mean 'arrogant,' Steven. Maybe this is just a matter of semantics. Maybe something else is bothering him. Maybe he was just tired," I suggested. "Whatever, give him some slack. This will work out. Trust me," I added with what I hoped sounded like confidence.

Looking up at the clock I realized that the first period bell was about to ring. "Class is going to start. You need to get going. I hope I helped, and I appreciate your coming to me," I said in a caring tone. "Whenever you need to talk to someone like this, I'm here. OK?"

Steven cracked an embarrassed smile. "OK. Thanks for listening," he said, initiating a firm handshake as the bell rang. "I'm gone," he added. And he was.

• ➤

Steven was gone, but my questions were not.

Did I come on too strong? Did I say too much to Steven? I wondered. Did I betray my earlier thoughts? And, more important, was my interest in Steven based solely on his possible homosexuality? Or was it based on something more general than that?

And again I had to ask myself, why was he coming to me? What did I represent to him that his friends or parents did not?

My mind-trip to Questionland was interrupted by Thuy Nguyen, a recent immigrant from Vietnam, who appeared at my door. It was time to do some work. Thuy sat across the desk from me and took from his notebook a list of words beginning with F. Its sound, unnatural to him, often was replaced with the sound of a P. "The funny, fat frog fit his food on the pire, I mean fire," he said tentatively.

"Fine!" I praised with a sly smile.

"Fine," he repeated, accenting the F.

Thuy's session ended fifteen minutes later. He departed, leaving the door wide open. I began entering my comments into Thuy's records when I sensed I was being watched.

I quickly looked up, through the gaping doorway. A dark figure stood across the hall, at the end of a row of lockers, staring at me. Shadows covered the form, but I could tell it was female. Her long hair was as dark as her shapeless black clothing. Her slouching posture was not particularly feminine and reflected poor self-esteem. From a distance, she looked like countless other girls at Columbia. As I looked up, I caught her in mid-stare. Her head jerked downward toward the book in her hands, as if she had been reading it all along. The reaction, however, betrayed her. The book was closed.

I turned away and faked adding additional comments to Thuy's record. With a quick movement, I looked up and through the doorway once more. The girl's head instantly tilted downward again. A pattern had been set.

That must be one fascinating book cover, I mused, focusing on my notes again. OK, young lady, that was two strikes. Three strikes and you're out.

I snapped my head in her direction a third time.

She was gone.

What was that all about? I wondered as the lunch bell split the day in half. Oh, wow, lunch already? I rhetorically asked the wall clock. Suddenly, I realized I hadn't even checked my mailbox that morning. I bolted from my office and rapidly marched down the hall. As I neared the main office, I noticed Steven and Brett talking at the end of the corridor. Spotting me, Steven inconspicuously flashed a brief "OK" sign. Brett did not notice. I nodded, acknowledging receipt of Steven's subtle signal, and with a wry smile on my lips, I thought, I did say 'This will work out. Trust me,' didn't I?

I quickly slid into the office, greeted the head secretary, Helen Woo, and reached for my mailbox handle. I pulled it toward me.

"Oh, my God," I gasped, looking into the tray. "There's no mail. I've never gone a whole day without getting any mail at work," I mumbled in Mrs. Woo's direction. "Oh, well, no news is good news. Right, Mrs. Woo?"

"Not necessarily, Mr. Lerner. Our photocopier is down. Maybe, you'll get some mail or a message later today."

Her prediction came true several hours later. As the end of the day neared, I could see, through my window, ominous purplish-gray clouds approaching.

There's a storm a-brewin' out there. Better get home as fast as I can. Gotta batten down the hatches, I silently joked, looking for an excuse to escape a little early.

I headed toward my car and immediately noticed unfamiliar splashes of bright color covering the parking lot, turning it into a con-crete artist's easel. Chalk artists had decorated the cement with a golden sunflower, a red "Cougars Rule," a blue peace symbol, a mul-ticolored bull's eye, and a white cross.

I meandered through a maze of letterman jackets, T-shirts, denim, and cigarette smoke hovering over the drawings and aimed for my car. Several heads turned, and their expressionless faces followed me as I sidestepped their Nike-covered feet.

"Who is that guy, anyway?" I heard a deep voice quietly ask. But before I heard an answer, I spotted the boldest, brightest piece of art in the lot. It was right behind my car. Covering the concrete directly in back of my assigned parking space was a large, chalky pink triangle.

I was able to gawk at it for only a moment before I heard the hushed laughter behind me.

Then, without warning, the dark clouds let loose a downpour onto the concrete art gallery at my feet. The stifled laughter behind me instantly became a series of rain-directed obscenities. I leaped into my car.

Was that pink triangle merely a copy, inspired by and mimicking the faded one on my bumper? I thought as I yanked my seat belt into position. Or was it supposed to menace me with its vividness and visibility? Was the triangular rose-colored splash created out of innocence or as a threat?

By the time I backed out of my slot, the deluge had scattered the teenagers and washed the pink triangle away, drowning it in a cement sea.

• ⤳

Several days passed before I saw Steven again. He peeked through my doorway one morning, before school, smiling.

"Hi, Mr. Lerner. How've you been?"

"Great. How about you?"

"Things are going well. I've just been real busy with homework, ASB, and running. There hasn't been much time for socializing. In fact, I'm heading to the library now. Just thought I'd pop in and say 'hi.'" And with that he disappeared.

That pretty much became Steven's routine over the next several months, right up to December's winter break. His quick visits were regular, although there was no real pattern to their frequency. Their purpose, it seemed, was merely to keep open the lines of communication. For the most part, these brief chats consisted of small talk, but occasionally the preppie young man would ask a pointed political question or make an observation about the state of the teen world around him.

"You know what really pisses me off about people around here?" he posed one day. "They're all so judgmental. People want everyone else to be just like themselves. And if they're not, they become marks for all sorts of crap," he observed. "I'm probably like that, too. But I'm working on it."

"It's not just kids. Adults can be pretty narrow-minded in their acceptance of others, too," I remarked, wondering what had triggered Steven's comments.

"Sometimes I just hear the stupidest things in these halls," he offered as a hint of explanation. "Anyway, I've got to get to the library. Take care."

That was typical of our "substantive" talks. They were short teasers, demanding more detail, more probing. If time allowed, I could have asked what he had heard. But I let Steven control the manner, methods, and situations in which we communicated.

If our relationship was a football game, then Steven would continue to be the quarterback, the playmaker, and I the receiver, just as we had been months before at the new staff presentation.

•⤳

It was the last school day prior to the two-week holiday break. The shockingly white December page on the wall calendar had been luring my restless eyes all day. Even with the thin black lines of the calendar grid and the scrawny numerals that filled the thirty-one boxes, the page radiated blankness. The brilliant red 25, however, stood out like Rudolph's nose against an Arctic snow field.

My eyes darted from the calendar to the digital clock on my desk. I glared at it. A seasonal green 1:59 stared back.

"Come on, bell," I ordered. "Ring." Several moments passed in silence. "Now!" I demanded impatiently. "There's a school full of antsy people who want to start Christmas break. I mean holiday break. They have things to do. Oh, to hell with them, bell. I want my vacation to start. Now. So ring, damn it."

Miraculously, the school bell obeyed, triggering the year-end early dismissal.

Instantly, Columbia High's halls became a tangle of students, without books, and teachers, with books, folders, and satchels, scurrying to exit academia and enter the whirlwind world of winter vacation. Within minutes, the building was empty except for a few administrators who had to stay. And me.

I had locked my office and walked, my rust-colored winter coat tucked under my arm, my gold-initialed brown briefcase dangling from my hand, to the teachers' lounge to make a phone call to my sister, confirming the family's holiday schedule.

The wobbly desk on which the smudged black phone rested sat next to a large window that overlooked Columbia's weather-worn dirt track. As I reached the desk, raised the receiver to my left ear, and pushed the sticky 9 button, I noticed a lone, darkly clad figure running on the far side of the oval course.

It was Steven.

I hung up the phone.

I had never seen Steven run before. Nor, for that matter, had I ever seen him in shorts, his legs exposed to the elements . . . and my eyes. His legs were ideal for long-distance running.

"Long, slender calf muscles," I observed before noticing the technique of Steven's stride or the speed of his steps. Then, as Steven sped along the back stretch of the track, my focus changed. I realized, even though I was not an expert on running, that I was watching a runner with a strong, studied mechanical kick, one with clockwork precision. I was impressed.

I knew nothing about the sport and had even less interest in it. That, actually, is an understatement. I resented running and runners. I had hated running since junior high when my P.E. class consisted almost entirely of running laps on an outdoor track, regardless of weather conditions. The teacher, a cold, colorless man named Preston, who served as track coach at a nearby high school, used running laps as both the primary class activity and as punishment for

not performing it well. His logic, or lack thereof, was that if one finished last in races around the track, extra laps would be run. I ran
countless extra laps.

To this day, I still hear Preston's gruff voice ridiculing me, humiliating me in front of my junior high classmates, never acknowledging
my sincere attempts to keep up with the other gym clothes–garbed
youths. All he seemed to notice was that I consistently finished last,
and placement appeared to be his only concern.

"What's the matter with you, Miss Lerner?" he would chide. "You
run like a girl. No, they run faster. They have to . . . to keep away
from the boys. Maybe that's it, Miss Lerner. You want the boys to
catch you. One more lap, loser girl. Maybe that'll teach you how to
be a man," Preston would taunt.

My experiences in his class instilled in me a resentment toward
running and anything associated with it that lasted into my adult-
hood. When jogging became a part of everyday American life in the
Seventies and Eighties, I stubbornly resisted the movement with the
fervor of a cat avoiding a bath. In fact, when I watch the Summer
Olympics, track and field coverage triggers instantaneous spasms of
channel surfing. I cannot watch that sport. It brings up too many
humiliating memories, too much pain from the past, and I knew, as
much as Steven Shepherd fascinated me, intrigued me, as talented a
track man as he was, I could never attend one of his races.

Steven had completed the curve at the far end of the oval and
was heading down the front straightaway, oblivious that my obser-
vant eyes were watching him from the lounge, when I noticed the
red COUGAR TRACK boldly printed across the chest of his black
fleece sweatshirt. As he ran by below my second-story vantage point,
I could see flecks of damp dirt spray from his Nike-covered heels,
splattering the back of his elongated calves. I also saw a red paw
print on the left buttock of his black cotton shorts, as well as three
more running up and across the back of his sweatshirt. At the top
of the sweatshirt, covering Steven's shoulder blades, red letters
punned COUGAR TRACKS.

As Steven chugged like a runaway train down the far side of the
oblong path, I watched in silent awe, hypnotized by the display of
determination, discipline, strength, and stamina. I could feel admira-

tion filling my soul, admiration and jealousy, as I admitted to myself the greatest shortcoming in my life, my failure to follow through, to stick with and even endure people and pastimes. I knew, then, that a second reason I could never attend Steven's track meets was that doing so would make me repeatedly face my painful failures.

Steven swung wide as he negotiated the distant arc of the track and then angled toward the building and began to slow down. As he approached my secret perch, I looked down and saw dark sweat stains around the neck of his shirt. I saw shiny perspiration matting his hair and coating his forehead, perspiration produced by an athlete's pain.

And I saw something else.

Steven's cheekbones glistened from moisture, too. But this sheen was not like that covering his scalp and brow. This wetness reflected a different kind of pain, the pain from within.

• ➤

When we returned to school in January, all the local media were buzzing with reports of the brutal New Year's Day murder of a local woman in her home. Summer Nelson, a history teacher at a nearby middle school allegedly had been bludgeoned to death by her brother. "The Lord told me 'Protect her from her evil lesbian lifestyle,'" he had claimed as he was arrested.

While I, as a gay man and teacher, probably had a more direct connection to this violent crime than the average citizen, I did not grasp how the Nelson murder would relate to Columbia High or affect me until I arrived at my office. Steven and Brett were waiting at the locked door, in silence.

"Well, what a surprise," I blurted, insensitive to their somber faces. "How was your vacation, guys?"

"Can we come in?" Steven asked, ignoring my question, as I unlocked the door. Together they entered, saucer-eyed yet expressionless.

"I can't believe Ms. Nelson's dead. She was the best teacher," Brett began. "She was our favorite," he tried to add before tears spilled down his cheeks.

I felt helpless. I knew I should have said something comforting, but I did not know Brett or Summer Nelson, nor did I understand their relationship. I looked at Steven, my confusion obvious.

"She was real special to us. She was a great teacher and a super nice person. She didn't deserve this," Steven eulogized in disbelief, as Brett's tears continued freely.

"There's little I can say right now, Brett, that'll make you feel better. I'm sorry," I apologized, for both Summer Nelson's death and my ineffective handling of his grief. "She sounds like a wonderful person. I wish I'd known her."

Steven, apparently more in control of his emotions, put a comforting supportive hand on his friend's shoulder, as Brett's crying ended. "Are you OK? I'm sure you can be excused from classes," soothed Steven. "It's OK if you don't want to be here today."

"Yeah, I'm OK now," responded Brett. "I'm just really embarrassed," he added as his cheeks reddened. "And I'm so damn mad at her brother. That bastard. I could just kill him."

"You don't mean that," Steven corrected his angry friend calmly.

"You don't know what I mean, Steven," Brett snapped. "I'm really pissed off at that asshole."

Realizing his vulgar choice of words, Brett's posture popped upright. "Oh, God, I'm sorry I said that, Mr. Lerner. I'm sorry I bothered you, but Steven said I could talk to you. He said if there was one person I could talk to, it would be you. Thanks, really. But I think I need to be alone." With that, Brett turned and fled the office, leaving Steven alone with me.

"Sometimes life just doesn't make sense, does it?" I asked rhetorically. Steven's silent response and downcast eyes told me that he understood that no answer was required. Besides, he probably did not have one.

"Steven," I spoke cautiously, knowing that what I was about to ask could be misinterpreted or deemed inappropriate. But I also knew that it was necessary.

For the first time, I had to be the quarterback. I had to take the snap and go on the offense.

"Could we meet sometime after school for a real talk? These quick chats we have seem to raise more questions than answers. At least for me. I think it's time we meet without looking at the clock and really complete a conversation. How does that sound?"

"I'd love it, Mr. Lerner," he replied with enthusiasm, his mood swinging upward immediately. "I'll be here Thursday . . . yeah Thursday, that's my free day . . . after school. Does that work for you?"

"Thursday, after school. Be here. Now have a decent day, and try not to dwell on Ms. Nelson, if you can," I consoled.

•⟶

All I had done was to become the quarterback. For one play. One play only. Every football team uses a trick play when necessary. So why was I feeling so guilty? Why was I feeling that what I had proposed might seem inappropriate or unprofessional to outsiders? Would they, or Steven himself, later perceive this as an attempt to seduce him when he was emotionally weakened by Summer Nelson's murder? Were these legitimate concerns? Or had I become unnecessarily paranoid? My mind raced through these questions as I desperately searched for answers and reasons for our relationship.

Suddenly one obvious answer leaped out at me, causing me to stop searching for any others. I had possessed the answer from the moment I first saw Steven, the moment he spiraled that football at my chest. It was at the base of all my feelings for Steven, and it cleared me of any guilt or confusion about my motives. Not once since that first vision of this unusual young man had I looked at him through lustful eyes. It was as simple as that. Regardless of what anyone assumed, regardless of my label, Steven simply was not my type. Although he was an attractive, enjoyable person, Steven's unfinished physicality did not arouse me. He was, after all, a teenager.

My motivation was something else: I was responding to Steven's implied request for me to be available, to listen, and, perhaps, help him sort out some ideas, fears, or feelings, whatever they were.

Having satisfactorily resolved that in my mind and finally understanding my role, my goal, in this situation, I had to formulate a game plan for Thursday. I would allow him to continue playing the quarterback, to control the direction of the conversation, but I would react to each pass he threw, each question he asked, with a lateral pass right back at him.

Perhaps, then, the specific reasons for his bonding with me would be made evident.

• ➤

By the time sixth period ended that Thursday, I was ready for Steven's visit. I had coached myself well. Receive each pass. Then return it with a lateral pass. It was game time. I had on my game face.

Steven arrived in my doorway less than five minutes after the final bell had rung. He was a bit out of breath, and his furrowed brow indicated some stress.

"Sorry I'm late," he needlessly apologized as I stacked the papers on my desk into one pile. "Some girl wanted to talk to me about the food in the lunchroom. Like I could do something about that." He took a deep breath. "Now what are we going to talk about?"

"Well, what do you want to talk about?" I lateraled his pass.

"Can we talk about Ms. Nelson? That was . . . is . . . really hard to take. You see, she was our favorite middle school teacher," he uttered, staring vacantly past me.

"May I ask why?" I pried.

"Well, in the seventh grade Brett and I were a lot alike. We dressed the same. We did everything together. We didn't have many other close friends. We had the same opinions on everything. Ms. Nelson noticed how inseparable we had become and told us that we were losing our identities. She taught us to explore ourselves, our differences, but to respect the differences in each other that we found. She told us that if we really were friends, the differences would not matter. And, you know, Mr. Lerner, what was so special about her? She talked to us as if we were adults, like you do."

Steven paused, exhaling a weak sigh. He had more to say. His eyes showed it. I did not interrupt.

"You know that stuff her brother said, about her being a lesbian," he said without hesitation, my ears exploding at the sound of the L word. "Do you think she talked to us about people's differences because she was a lesbian?"

"Well, I don't know, Steven," I answered, stunned that he had brought this up so easily. "The only way we could know that would be to ask her. And we can't. Maybe she was just a sensitive person who appreciated your close friendship with Brett."

"She probably was my first gay friend," Steven surmised pensively.

My God, I thought in shocked silence. What is he saying? Was he so aware of the number of gay people in society that he realized that it was inevitable to have some as friends? Or was he saying that as a gay person it was inevitable that he have gay friends? Or was he just testing me?

"No. Wait. Lynne probably was my first gay friend," he corrected himself. "Actually, she was my older sister's friend. They were kind of like Brett and me. When Lynne went to Claremont College in California, she wrote my sister a letter telling her that she had become a lesbian. Well, my sister couldn't handle it. She said she didn't actually dislike Lynne, but she just didn't want her as a friend anymore." Then Steven added with a weak laugh. "Maybe my sister should have had a talk with Ms. Nelson!"

I joined his laughter. But inside I was not laughing. The irony of this conversation was making me feel quite uncomfortable. Here was a high school student freely discussing lesbians with a gay male faculty member who couldn't speak as freely because it might jeopardize his job. But an even bigger irony was that while I had gotten my wish—to be an "ear or shoulder" for a student—I totally failed to understand why it had happened with this particular individual.

Our conversation meandered through several subjects, just brushing some, getting to the core of others. Then I remembered one topic I had intended to discuss.

"Steven, we've never really addressed something I learned about from the interview in The Chronicle last fall. Your military plans.

What's up with that?" I asked calmly, trying to hide my feelings regarding the military and military personnel in general.

"Well," he retorted quickly, "like I said, it is a little about patriotism and a little about the financial gain, but I think it is a lot more about the challenge. The way I look at it, Mr. Lerner, if I can survive boot camp and anything else the army throws at me, I can deal with any situation in my life."

"I can't argue with that, Steven," I concurred. "I'm sure you've thought this out, and I do trust your judgment. I just hope you never face a situation more difficult than boot camp," I told him.

As our talk wound down, Steven asked some general questions about my high school days. He knew that I, too, had been a student leader and asked how I had dealt with the responsibilities, pressures, and image of being one. Then he asked, in an embarrassed manner, how I dealt with the issues of conformity, drugs, and alcohol. He did not include sex, but I think he wanted to. His questions were cautiously vague and protectively general. So were my answers.

"Steven," I reminded him, "I'm from a different generation. Some of the issues you've mentioned have remained the same through time. Some definitely have not. How would I advise you to handle these serious subjects? I'd tell you to listen to yourself, that you'll hear the answers. Trust yourself. Know yourself. Respect yourself. Love yourself."

We sat in silence for a moment, as Steven visibly contemplated my words.

"This is a perfect point on which to end this conversation," I concluded. "We've covered a lot of territory. We can always pick it up from here later if you want. You're welcome here any time."

I stopped there, realizing Steven's eyes were focused directly on mine. "Thanks, I appreciate that," he said sincerely. The intensity of his look reflected a need for me to make one more risky offer.

"In fact, if you ever find yourself in trouble or have a problem, and it is something you're not yet ready to go to your parents with, don't be afraid to call me at home." I smiled. "Just one promise, though. No crank calls!"

Steven burst into laughter. The joke was not that funny. He simply needed to release the tension and emotion that had built up.

"Yeah, like I still make crank calls," he offered as he rose from the office chair, extending his hand.

He stepped to the open door and turned to face me. "It's really cool having you for a friend, Mr. Lerner." Then he spun around and bounced down the hall. I sat motionless, mesmerized, for a long while.

• ✐

That conversation lingered with me for days. The ease with which Steven talked about serious issues, often personal issues, with me, an adult, continued to mystify me. His facial expressions, those eyes that appeared both direct and secretive at the same time, haunted me. The words and phrases Steven chose seemed to reflect thoughts and feelings far deeper than their face value. Either they had a secret meaning or I had a vivid imagination.

For many weeks after that meeting, our talks returned to their previous pattern and content. Regular and brief, the dialogues touched a variety of subjects. Often they seemed to offer Steven a safe place to vent anger, irritation, or disappointment in someone or something. Occasionally, he would whet my curiosity by inadvertently divulging clues about himself.

I learned from these brief chats, for example, that Steven spent considerable time reading. That really did not surprise me. However, when he added that he often drove up the Columbia River Gorge to read, to think, to walk along the water, the loner inside Steven became more evident.

Although popular and active, somehow Steven felt alone in the world. He was, in that manner then, just like many other teenagers.

As April 1 neared, announcements regarding the April Fool's Tolo, a Columbia High tradition, appeared in the daily bulletins as well as on butcher-paper posters in the hallways. Well, this is one dance Steven won't be missing; I'll bet girls are already lining up to ask him, I thought as I looked at one of the signs. Then, like the rays of sunrise sneaking over the distant landscape, it dawned on me that in all our exchanges Steven had never mentioned a girlfriend. He had not even mentioned going out on a date.

Isn't this interesting? I mused to myself. I'll have to find a subtle way to bring this up the next time he drops by.

Steven did not drop by again until after the Tolo, which gave me a logical excuse to bring up the subject.

"I've been meaning to ask you," I began as he peeked into my office one morning, "if you went to the Tolo."

"Oh, sure," he responded without any excitement. "I went with Jonna Higgins. She's just a friend. Do you know who she is?" he inquired. I shook my head negatively. "She's captain of the girls' track team."

"You know," I said, continuing my investigation, "I've never asked you where you like to go when you go out. In fact, I don't think you've ever mentioned dating."

"Oh, I date sometimes. But I really can't afford it. Besides, I usually do things in groups," he explained with a self-conscious laugh. "Hey, the bell's going to ring! See you later," Steven noted conveniently, as he turned and ran.

Rarely did Steven appear uncomfortable talking to me. This, however, had been one of those occasions. How interesting! I thought.

• ⟋

April and May were busy months for Steven, myself, and all the other captives at Columbia High. Track team workouts and meets took much of Steven's time every spring. But this year with student elections, rally squad selections, meetings, and classes also putting extra demands on him, Steven found very little time for himself. Even I found the twenty-four-hour day to be too short as workshops and committee meetings filled my days. As a result, I saw relatively little of young Mr. Shepherd, and I feared my time to put together this teenage puzzle was running out. He would be graduating soon and entering the military, leaving me without any conclusions, just suspicions, as to why we had bonded as we had.

Quite unexpectedly, I ran into Steven at a coffee shop near school one mid-May afternoon. A long meeting with the English-as-a-second-language teachers had kept me late. Steven, hair still wet, had just showered off an hour of laps. I was feeling drained and needed a caffeine cure. Apparently, Steven did, too.

"Young man," I sarcastically accused as I sneaked up behind him at the counter, "you're too young to drink coffee."

Recognizing my voice, he turned, gave an innocent smile, and, feigning a childish voice, defended himself: "My mom says I can!"

I coughed up a short laugh. "How's track?" I questioned, after a brief pause.

"Fine," Steven assured me. "State finals are this weekend. My times have been around last year's, so I could win again. I'm trying to peak at the meet and break my own record," he said, psyching himself with an athlete's confidence.

"I know you will," I predicted positively as we looked for a place to sit.

Moments later, as we sat at the white wrought-iron table in front of the store, sipping our coffee, an awkwardness filled me. This was our first meeting not held in my office or at a school event. When we met in my office, the door was always ajar, if not open wide. When we talked at school events, witnesses swirled around us.

This accidental off-site meeting, on the other hand, had no connection to school. It could be perceived as a secret rendezvous.

"Let's walk back to the school and drink our coffee on the lawn,"
I suggested. "If someone from school sees us here, they . . ."

" . . . might think it strange," he finished my sentence. "I understand. I've got a reputation, too, you know. What will people say if
they see me hanging with a teacher?" he joked rising from his seat.

As Steven and I headed toward the school, I observed that I had
not seen much of him. "You've been a pretty busy guy. Besides running, what have you been up to?"

"A lot. Maybe too much," Steven replied. "There are a lot of things
to fit in. And now senior class activities are beginning to happen.
Mom says the only time she sees me nowadays is at dinner, if I eat
with them."

Steven had thrown me a perfect opportunity to ask about his family. He rarely mentioned them. I knew next to nothing about his home
life. I tossed my question at him: "Tell me about your folks, Steven."

"What do you want to know?" he asked openly. "My dad is a
lawyer. Mom is the secretary at my old grade school. My sister,
Crystal, is studying business at University of Portland. She's three
years older than me."

"That sounds like a great family," I noted. He nodded. "I hope you
appreciate what you've got."

"Oh, I do. Believe me," Steven responded.

"Are you close to your parents?" I pried.

"I guess so. I think I'm closer to mine than most kids are to theirs.
We do talk to each other about stuff," he detailed.

"Do you consider them your friends?" I asked, hoping his answer
would help tell me why he had needed me as a friend.

"Yes, of course," Steven replied rapidly, almost defensively. Then
pausing, he looked down thoughtfully and said, "No, not exactly.
They're my parents, not friends. I don't really think of them as friends.
You get to choose your friends."

Gazing directly at me, he inquired, "Do you consider your parents
your friends?"

"Now I do. I certainly didn't at your age," I revealed. "but we
became friends."

"I've never thought about this before. That's one of the things I like about talking to you, Mr. Lerner. You make me think about things," he confessed, not realizing how his words were pieces to a puzzle I had been trying to complete for months.

"Do you respect your parents? Trust them? Listen to them? Love them?" I tested.

"Well, sure I do!" snapped Steven.

"Good," I snapped back. "I guess that's what I really wanted to hear. Then, you'll be friends. Hey," I changed the subject, "this year is almost over! You're almost history. And the prom is just a couple of weeks away. You are going, aren't you?"

"Yeah. I'm taking Lisa Barrett. I know her from church. She goes to Hood Vista High," he informed me. "She's a real nice girl."

"That's cool," I interjected.

"But, you know, I'm not really looking forward to it," he announced matter-of-factly. "Once the state track meet is over, I wish I could just take my diploma and disappear. I'm ready to get out of this place."

I was disappointed, saddened, by Steven's revelation. I would have expected him to delight in all the graduation activity that culminated his years of leadership, involvement, and hard work.

"Why would you say something like that?" I reacted, obviously surprised by his disillusionment.

"Since I've been here, I've given all I could," Steven sighed. "I think I've just burned out. I think I've just burned out being Steven Shepherd," he clarified in a tired tone. "And it still isn't enough! They wanted me to be a commencement speaker. I told them to give some-body else a chance. They couldn't believe that I said 'no.' But it was not really about giving somebody else a chance. I was just tired of being Steven Shepherd, the perfect guy you can always count on. I wanted to show them that I have a chink in my armor. I'm allowed to have a chink in my armor, aren't I?" he asked angrily without wait-ing for an answer. "I'm just ready to get out of here and go to boot camp where nobody knows who I've been or who I am," he said, con-tinuing his frustrated rant.

"I don't know what to say," I fumbled. "How long has this been brewing inside you?"

"Several weeks. Months," he answered weakly.

"You've been keeping this to yourself for several months?" I shot back. "Have you talked to anyone about this?"

"No."

"Not even Brett?" I asked sharply.

"No."

"Do you remember our conversation a while back?" I asked, quieting my voice. "I told you to come to me if you were in trouble or had a problem. Why didn't you talk to me about this?"

"This isn't your problem."

"You're right, this isn't my problem. But, as unusual as it is, we've become friends. Right? We are friends, aren't we?"

"Well, sure."

"OK, then. Friends share. Friends care. I care. Friends talk. You should have talked to me. Jesus Christ, you're almost there, Steven. You're almost out," I said, my volume gradually rising. "Then you can be a different Steven Shepherd if you want, if you feel trapped. But I don't think you'd be that much different a man than you are now. And I think you should be damn proud of that man. Hell, you should be proud of whoever you are!" I said too loudly for the private nature of our conversation. I paused. "I'm sorry for yelling. Just remember, next time you need my ear, talk to me."

Steven nodded silently, humbled, but not humiliated, by my words.

"It's nearly five. We've got to get moving," I noted, trying to change the mood. "I hope you heard what I said. I meant it. Now, good luck at the state meet. You'll do great," I said, punching him on the bicep. "I won't be there physically, Steven. I'm driving up to Seattle for the weekend. My mom turns sixty-five Sunday. But I'll be with you in thought."

"That's cool," Steven responded. "Running is my thing. It's not yours."

"That's for sure," I agreed. "But I'll be with you in thought," I repeated.

We rose in unison, turned, and went our separate ways. Several steps later, I peeked over my shoulder in Steven's direction just in time to catch him sneaking a quick glance at me. It was accompanied by a smile, a smile of contentment.

•➤

When I arrived at school Monday morning, a long banner hung across the main hall. "Congratulations, Steven Shepherd! Champ Sets Record Again!" it read in bold red letters.

All right! I reacted inside my head. You did it. Now the pressure is off. You don't have to be the perfect Steven Shepherd anymore. You can deal with the chink in your armor!

I stepped into the main office to get my mail and began to stride happily down the hall to my office.

"Mr. Lerner!" Steven called from behind me, as he ran to catch up.

"Congratulations!" I greeted him, beaming, as our free hands met in a high-five.

"Remember our talk last week," he said with a grin as wide as the mouth of the Columbia River. "Well, I felt better the minute I left you. I felt like, this is so dumb, a weight was lifted off me and I was able to focus on my race," he confided in hushed tones. "Without that weight, I felt like I could fly. And I guess I did. So, thanks. Really!"

"I'm very happy for you," I responded cheerily. "Now you've only got a few weeks left. Enjoy them. They'll be over before you know it, Champ."

He walked away smiling. So did I.

As I entered my office I began thumbing through my mail. A note from Anna Lewis, the activity coordinator, was on top. "Tim," it read, "some chaperons for this Saturday's prom have canceled. Could you help out?"

I had plans to spend the weekend with friends at Cannon Beach on the coast, but they could be changed. Impulsively, I decided to chaperon the prom. Intuitively I knew there was a reason for my being there.

I saw Steven briefly twice that week, scurrying between classes. I didn't stop to mention my unexpected prom duties. As he passed me though, I could hear him mumble something under his breath, as if it were for my ears only.

"Tick, tick, tick" is what I thought I heard.

The first time I heard it, I laughed. He's counting down the minutes until graduation, I surmised.

The second time I heard the ticking, it seemed to have more urgency. More like a time bomb. I peered over my shoulder, frightened by my own thoughts, as Steven walked away, stepping to the cadence of a manic second-hand.

No, I reprimanded myself. Don't even think it!

• ⤳

Prom night arrived in a hurry. I frantically fought through the hanger jungle in my closet looking for my rarely worn, dark gray suit. It was deep in the thickest thicket, abandoned. I took my one long-sleeved white shirt and ironed it. I selected a floral print tie in shades of yellow, golds, and reds after studying its contrasting bright colors against the dark suit. I pinned on a white carnation boutonniere. I even shined my shoes.

"When," I mused as I knotted the flowery cravat, "was the last time I shined my shoes? Hell, when was the last time I went to a prom?"

I entered the elegant downtown hotel's palatial ballroom an hour early as I had been instructed. Immediately I impatiently began scanning the foyer every few seconds hoping to find Steven. But the first formally clad couples did not arrive for more than an hour.

And Steven did not arrive until an hour after that. His traditional black tuxedo, with a red bow tie and cummerbund, suited him perfectly, reflecting his conservative but dynamic nature and emphasizing his long lines and erect posture. A red carnation boutonniere adorned his lapel. Steven had chosen to wear red and black, his school colors, to the prom.

My first vision of Steven as he stepped through the doors into the stylish ballroom virtually pierced my heart. For, although I had known him less than a year, I felt as if he had been a part of my life much longer. Seeing him, framed by the light in the doorway, I also felt as if he had grown up before my eyes.

My feelings for this exceptional young man somehow had become that of a proud father, or perhaps, more appropriately, unofficial godfather. I stared at him, silently thanking his parents for creating such a fine person and hoping they would not be threatened by the unusual bond that had developed between their son and myself.

And I thanked Steven for teaching me something I never expected to learn about myself, that I had never even seriously considered.

"I would have made one hell of a father!" I announced joyfully to myself.

My attention then turned to the young woman next to Steven. "That must be Lisa. She's absolutely . . . ," I searched for the exact word, " . . . sweet." Wholesome, blonde, and blue-eyed, she was the picture of innocence and sweetness in her plain powder-blue full-length gown. Her golden hair fell into a simple pageboy style. She was attractive in a nonthreatening way. She was like many of the girls I had dated in high school and college a generation before. She was a "safe" date.

It was obvious to me why Steven had asked Lisa to the prom. She would not have any sexual expectations of him. Nor would he feel pressure to violate his personal moral code. After all, they knew each other from church. Her pleasant appearance and simple manner implied that merely going out with a young man as nice, decent, respected, and popular as Steven was exciting. It was sufficient.

Steven had not seen me yet, peering through the tuxedos and elegant evening gowns. I could see him awkwardly guiding Lisa into the room, greeting classmates and introducing them to his cheery companion. And companions is exactly what they were. Their body language said "friends." It did not indicate romance. It did not have "chemistry."

The mingling well-dressed crowd parted, and I was visible to Steven for the first time. His eyes locked on mine. While pride filled my eyes, relief filled his. He stepped toward me, reaching for Lisa as an afterthought.

"I didn't know you'd be here," he spurted in surprise. "And look at you. I've never seen you in a suit and tie before. Not bad, Mr. Lerner. Not bad," he assessed.

"Look at me? Look at you," I returned the volley. "Why you even had enough class to wear black dress shoes with your tuxedo! I expected to see your brown top-siders!"

Then Steven introduced me to Lisa, and we made cordial formal dance chitchat. But as we talked, Steven's eyes seemed to say something secretly to me. I could not hear it very clearly, but I think it was "Get me out of here!"

• ➤

I was right. Early Monday morning, Steven stood in my office doorway. "Yes, I had a nice time," he said, answering my unasked question as I looked up. "But I sort of wish I hadn't gone. Don't ask me why, though, 'cuz I can't say yet."

"OK, I won't," I obeyed. "But do you know how handsome . . . no, dignified . . . no, presidential you looked Saturday night?"

"Give me a break," Steven pleaded in embarrassment. "I know it was supposed to be an important event in my life. And it was, I guess. I'm just glad you were a part of it. Thanks for being there."

"Well, don't think I was there for you, Kid," I said, jokingly. "I was there to make sure no one puked on anybody, dropped illegal substances into the punch bowl, or got into a food fight."

"Thanks again for being there," he repeated, seeing through my joke. "Tick, tick, tick. Two more weeks and counting," he announced as he headed for his locker down the hall.

Steven's comfort with our relationship, the openness of his confidences, and his relaxed manner seemed to have reached a new level during the past several weeks. He, too, it seemed, had noted that time was running out.

I hoped that's what his "tick, tick, tick" meant.

• ➤

On Wednesday afternoon, the yearbook was distributed. A young lady with royal blue hair and considerably more earrings than ears brought mine. Steven's picture appeared throughout the annual, much to his humiliation, I'm sure. My favorite was a candid shot taken at a football game. Steven, sitting on Brett's shoulders, wore one of the rally girl's puffy red pompoms as a hat.

Inserted into the back of the yearbook was the "Last Will and Testament of the Class of '90," in which seniors bequeathed to other students, faculty, friends, and family a variety of personal items, memories, and wishes, often in the form of private jokes. Thumbing through the alphabetized list, I found Steven's will. I will never forget how it read.

It contained coded, mysterious bequests to a number of people, most of whom I did not know. Near the end of the list, however, I recognized a name.

"To the Weiss Guy," it simply read, "I leave my youth . . . and my love."

What a touching sentiment, I thought as my eyes lingered a moment on his words to Brett. Then I read on to Steven's final gift.

"To T.L.," I read as my eyes, heart, and brain collided with the page. "Thanks for being there even when I wasn't. Thanks for listening to me. But more important, thanks for hearing me. You showed me the way. For that, I bequeath my eternal friendship."

Thank God I was alone in my office when I read his message to me, because tears exploded uncontrolled from my eyes. I leaped from my desk to shut the door, kicking the wastebasket across the room in my haste. I read the will over several times in proud disbelief, my tears flowing uninterrupted.

Suddenly I realized I had been successful. It was official. Steven had confirmed that. I had reached out my hand; I had offered my shoulder to a student; I had been an ear to Steven, and I had helped him. Yet, I still was not certain why or how. Until my questions were answered, Steven, our relationship, and its effect on him would remain a puzzle to me.

I wanted to pull Steven aside and directly ask my obsessive questions before the school year ended, but I could not, because it, plain and simple, was up to him to say the words. I could not lead the witness. I could not pressure him. I could not make him say what he was not yet ready to say. Besides, I could not find him.

With just a few days left, Steven, like the other seniors, was running helter-skelter signing annuals, studying for tests, rehearsing the commencement ceremony, and trying to cope with the flurry of activity during his final moments at Columbia.

But the flurry of activity did not restrain one mysterious senior from reappearing. Just prior to graduation day, another pink triangular note was placed among my mail. Luckily, I did not notice it until I had returned to my office.

"I really wish I had had the guts to talk to you this year," it read in the identical boldface type that had adorned the first note. "I know I could have. I know I should have. There's just so much risk involved. No one here would understand. No one at home would understand. I just want to get away from these people and be me. Thank you for showing me that I can. Thank you for being a pink triangle."

I stared in stunned silence at the sad note, gradually looking heavenward. "God," I prayed, "please, look after this one. He or she is in pain and needs your help."

For the remainder of the day, I felt a weight on my shoulders, a sadness. I dwelled on the note, on the difficult time the writer was having, on the loneliness expressed. I hoped tomorrow's graduation ceremony would release the young person into a world of self-discovery, self-acceptance, and happiness.

• ✦

By the time Friday's graduation arrived, a feeling of completion had filled the campus and spread to the downtown auditorium where the ceremony would take place. The faces, as well as the words, of students, parents, and faculty alike, expressed a combination of pride and relief as they entered the hall.

The moment *Pomp and Circumstance* began and the Class of '90 slowly filed into the arena and to their seats, my mind became a blur. My eyes sped up and down the queue of black-and-red-gowned graduates-to-be looking for Steven. Finally, I found him, his unique proud posture setting him apart from the other ebony-draped young men. Like a magnet, my gaze was fixed on him, looking away only to blindly search for the mystery senior, the pink triangle.

I heard the commencement speakers, the Cambodian refugee girl and the football team captain, give their talks about the memories of the past and the challenges of the future, but I did not truly listen. I sat in a world of my own thoughts, questions, memories, and challenges. I wondered if some of Steven's thoughts, questions, memories, and challenges interlocked with mine. And I wondered who my mystery confidant was. And I knew that I must stop obsessing on all this for it soon would be over.

I did not notice when the school board president began her general comments and generic congratulatory remarks, nor did I see Principal Gregory Grimm join her at the podium as the first row of the four-hundred-plus seniors stood to receive their diplomas. My thoughts had drifted from the present, filled with Steven and the unknown burgeoning pink triangle, to my painful past nearly twenty-five years before.

Perhaps it was the warm mugginess generated by the hundreds of bodies in the poorly air-conditioned auditorium, but somehow I was returned to the late August heat wave just prior to my senior year back home in Seattle . . .

• ⤳

I was cruising the University of Washington campus on my black Schwinn; my tie-dyed tank top and cutoffs clung to me like damp newspaper. There were no clouds. There was no breeze, a rare occurrence in Seattle. Ahead of me rose Husky Stadium. Next to it, at the end of a sloping patchwork of green and yellow lawn, Lake Washington calmly lay, gleaming, glaring, blinding me with daggers of reflected light. Peeking over the verdant distant suburban foothills across the water, were mountains, the Cascades, pressing their palms to the heavens, holding up the perfectly painted blue sky.

The bicycle path curved toward the looming football stadium, drawing passers-by over the top of the hill away from the grassy slope. I was alone. There was no one around. But there was an aging, run-down, red-brick public bathroom perched near the shoreline at the foot of the long, sloping lawn.

The bathroom, as legend had it, was where homosexuals—*perverts, queers, cocksuckers*—went to have sex. It was one of those legends that permeate a high school, that titillate the imagination, the libido, the testosterone-laden bodies of teenage boys. The story of the university student who found two bloodied fat, old naked men dead on the cold concrete floor curled in mutual fellatio was ageless. No one knew where the story had come from. No one knew the student's name. No one could offer any proof. No one ever questioned any of the details, the logic of the story. Yet the legend lived on, and the building became known as "the campus can."

You didn't want to be caught near "the campus can."

Yet there I was, mysteriously drawn to it anyway, staring curiously from the hilltop in the humid August heat. And I had to go to the bathroom.

I looked around. I saw no witnesses. I coasted down the slope on my Schwinn, circling the building once, stopping behind it, between it and the glistening lake, hidden from the vantage point above. I leaned my bike against the discolored, disintegrating brick wall; inhaled slowly, deeply, shakily; and entered.

A horizontal strip of glass formed a window high on the wall, just under the ceiling, allowing just enough light in to cover the room in a grayish haze, the same gray as the cold concrete walls and floor. The room was cool, protected from the outside heat by its thick concrete armor. One exposed light bulb shone dimly from the far wall. There was a urinal and one doorless stall.

I quickly stepped to the stained, dripping urinal, unzipped my cutoffs, and began to pee.

"Hurry," I ordered myself, "before someone comes in."

And then I saw it, out of the corner of my eye, on the wooden wall that divided the urinal from the stall. It was writing, finely scrawled into the wood, barely visible in the gray light:

Blow jobs 9:00 Tues

Today's Tuesday, I realized, as my heart began pounding. I zipped up and hastily stepped out into the heavy summer afternoon, grabbing my bike and pushing it back to the hilltop vista as fast as I could. I didn't even turn around when I got there, but just briefly looked back over my shoulder at the frightening, yet intriguing, little building. I hopped on the Schwinn and peddled directly home.

Maybe that story is true, I admitted as I sprawled across my bed looking at the closed gold and brown striped curtains that kept the five o'clock sun from my room. Guys do get sucked-off in there, I conceded in disbelief. But what kind of guys? Are they all perverted weirdoes? I wondered. Or are some of them like . . . me?

Lying on my pulled-back sheets, my cutoffs sticking to me in the trapped wet warmth of my room, I reread the graffiti etched in my mind, re-experienced my visit to "the campus can." Who would write something like that? I questioned. What would he look like? Do people do it right there? Shit, that's just plain gross!

The mental whirlwind of questions and visualizations continued, my imagination triggering questions I had never dared ask myself before. How would something like that feel? Finally, I challenged myself with the ultimate unspeakable, unthinkable question: Could I do that? I posed, probably revealing more than I intended.

It was then I realized I was aroused. My erection pressed at my fly. I was breathing hard. I leaped from the matted linens, disgusted with myself, and lunged toward the curtains, snapping them open, hoping the attacking brightness would shock my groin into relaxation. It did.

But throughout dinner that evening, as my mother and year-younger sister, Debbie, quibbled over the appropriate length of girls' shorts and Dad silently read *The Seattle Times* sports section, I planned my return to the deserted grassy slope. When dinner was over and I had cleared the dishes from the table, I self-consciously announced, "I'm stuffed. I'm going to ride around for a while."

As I arrived at the viewpoint above the isolated public toilet, dusk was beginning to bathe the lower UW campus, transforming the adjoining lake waters into a flat sheet of liquid steel and turning the Cascades into a dark purple curtain. I stood straddling the Schwinn, leaning lightly on my handlebars, trying to focus down the long, sloping lawn. No one appeared to be down there.

Fifteen minutes passed. The dimness of dusk grew deeper. I still could not see anyone in the area. I did not hear any voices, either. No footsteps. No rustling vegetation. I was alone.

Slowly, nervously inching forward toward the darkening structure, I noticed the narrow slit of light leaking from the building near the roofline.

How bright can that light bulb be? I asked myself as I moved around to the bathroom's back side and leaned my bike against the broken brick wall, near the doorway to the men's room.

I took a silent, unsteady breath, licked my dry lips, wriggled my fingers trying to free the nervousness from them, looked straight ahead, and walked through the door into the cool room. The lone low-watt light told me that no one else was there.

Fuck! I exclaimed in a mix of disappointment and anger. What a bust! All this worry and sweat for nothing. I stepped closer to the wooden wall next to the urinal, bent over slightly to reread the shadowy writing, to make certain I had read it correctly.

Suddenly, I noticed a pair of silent white tennis shoes close behind me. Before I had a chance to stand up, a rigid, cupped hand forcefully covered my mouth. The other hand grabbed around my waist, trapping my arm against my side, trying to yank open the snap and zipper of my cutoffs. I could tell the person was taller and considerably broader than me.

"I'm gonna fuck your ass, you little perv. That's what you really want anyway," he told me in a more matter-of-fact than threatening manner. "Jayce, watch the damn door! Don't let anyone near here or I'll kill ya," he ordered an invisible partner, as I tried to struggle. But my arms were pinned against my sides, my mouth covered, lips pressed painfully against my teeth, and my nose was blocked by the top of his index finger. Somehow, he'd already managed to get my torn denim shorts and underwear down to my knees, eliminating my ability to kick well. His success in rendering me helpless was not an accident. The choreography had been planned. He was experienced at this.

"Came here for a blow job, didn't you?" he menaced. "Well, I ain't no cocksuckin' queer."

I tried to turn my head slightly to get a glimpse of his face, but his dominant strength forced me to keep my eyes forward.

"Don't even think of looking at me or you'll be kissing this wall hard, real hard!" he warned. "Besides, you want this. So, relax, Faggot, and take it like a man."

How he managed to undo his jeans remains a mystery to me. My attacker did not seem limited by having only two hands. They were everywhere. And then the inevitable reality that his hands were not my greatest concern set in. Using his height, bulk, and strength, he began forcing me to bend over, and I could feel something jabbing my asshole. My already tense body tightened even more, my ass clenching shut, trying to block his hard cock from penetrating. But his position of power was too dominant and with one brutally violent thrust he violated my body, my soul, my life.

The pain was unlike anything I had ever felt before, tearing deep into my bowels. Muffled moans escaped my smothered mouth, causing him to press his hand harder against my lips and teeth. I stood on tiptoes, trying to flee the excruciating pain, the horror, the indignity. But there was nowhere to flee. I was face-to-face with the graffiti-covered wooden wall. Through a teary blur *Blow jobs 9:00 Tues* stared at me, witnessing my rape, as I groaned in agony.

"I said 'Take it like a man,'" the rapist repeated. "Now comes the good part," he added, beginning the first of what I feared would be countless piercing thrusts. But after only a few rapid motions, perhaps four or five, his quickened breathing indicated that orgasm was close.

After two more sharp pushes he stopped moving, slightly relaxing his grip on my mouth and loosening the vise that held my right arm against my side and abdomen.

No vocal noises accompanied his orgasm, just the whooshing sounds of air forced through clenched teeth.

Stinging, biting, burning fire seared my rectal opening as he pulled out with a jolting snap. The agony of penetration, the pain of his rough thrusts, was replaced with the aching aftermath of trauma, like the lingering smart of a slap across the face. But, thank God, he was out. I exhaled slowly.

"Don't look at me!" he ordered. "Eyes on the wall," his directions continued, as he released me from his tight clasp, pulled up his jeans, and closed them.

"Jayce," he whispered roughly, "get in here! It's your turn."

My heart sank to the concrete below me. Not again. Please, not again, I pleaded to myself. What did I do to deserve this? I asked. How much more of this hell must I endure?

A second set of sneakers stepped silently into the barely lit room. "He's waiting for ya, Jayce. See, he's already got his pants down," my belligerent menace said with a laugh, pushing a hand into the small of my back, pressing me in place against the wood partition. "Here. Take him. He's yours."

But as he shoved me forward, he turned me slightly to the side, allowing the camera in my eye a flash image. But it was enough for me to see his strawlike hair, sharp profile, and robust frame in the weak shaft of light leaking from the light bulb on the far wall.

Remember what you saw. There's something familiar about him, I told myself, as he exchanged places with his partner, exiting into the still night.

"I'm gonna have a cigarette, Man. You better be done by the time I'm finished with it," he threatened through the open door.

Jayce now held me against the wall with a forearm across my shoulder blades. But his pressure was not as forceful as that of his predecessor. And he did not cover my mouth. Instead, his left hand grabbed my shoulder, cupping it almost tenderly, and pulled me from the wall, closer to him. I sensed he was about my size.

"I'm not gonna fuck you, Man. OK? We're gonna fake this so he thinks we did it," he instructed in a soothing, almost inaudible whisper. "I'm sorry about this. Really sorry. But no one fucks with him, if they want to live. Believe me. I know," he went on. I could feel my body, both inside and out, relaxing as Jayce spoke. And as he spoke, Jayce caressed my shoulder.

"I'm just gonna jack off. I'd like you to try, too. If you can't right now, well, I'll understand," he continued, presenting his bizarre plan. I heard the pop of his frayed Levi's 501 cutoffs opening, as his left hand moved smoothly from my shoulder to inside my tank top, toying with my left nipple. I could feel the rhythm of his right hand as he began to stroke himself behind me.

No one had ever touched my nipple, touched me like that. No one had ever talked to me, whispered to me, as softly as he had. So, weird as it sounds, considering what I had just gone through, I became aroused.

Perhaps it was because I was so vulnerable right then, desperate for any kind words, any loving touches. I don't know. All I know is that my heart raced with passion. I voluntarily leaned against him, allowing his left arm to hold me as he continued manipulating my nipple. His hand slowly, sensually slid down to my cock, discovering its stiff state.

"Good," Jayce approved quietly, as he tilted his head to kiss and lick my neck. I could feel shoulder-length hair drag across my skin, and I could hear his breath gaining speed. He firmly held my cock in his left hand. No one had ever done that before. He began to stroke it while his right hand palmed his own organ.

Maybe it was the newness of the experience. Maybe it was my confusion. Maybe it was my subconscious way of thanking him for not hurting me. Maybe it was merely my teenage horniness, or my long-held fantasy of a man's loving touch, but I was extremely aroused, nearing orgasm with very little effort. In fear, I tried to remove his hand from my erect shaft.

"No," he breathed, "let it happen. I'm gonna shoot," his voice quivered.

Two strokes later, Jayce lurched, groaning and gasping, spewing his cum over the curve of my right buttock. At precisely the moment I felt his warm semen, I erupted against the wall, making sounds I'd never been allowed to make in the privacy of my room.

Our bodies relaxed as one. His left arm, still encircling my torso, loosened slightly, his hand lightly rubbing my chest. His tongue slid from the nape of my neck to my earlobe.

"I'm almost done with my cigarette, Jayce. You'd better be done in there," the rapist announced from outside, reminding us of his omnipotent presence.

"Yeah," responded Jayce. Then in a hushed voice he said to me, as we tugged our pants into position, "I gotta get outa here. He's ready to split. But, listen, take a hot bath when you get home. For your ass. For your head, too. You'll feel better. And I'm really sorry. You'll be OK, though."

He stepped to the door. "You know, you could've looked at me. I would have let you," he whispered, escaping into the night before I had an opportunity to look.

"OK, let's go," I heard Jayce mumble from the other side of the concrete wall. "Can I have a cigarette, Rick? Please," he asked timidly as his voice faded into the night.

I waited a moment, peeked out the door into the darkness, saw that they had left, grabbed my bike, and peddled away as fast as I could.

My thoughts spun in circles as I raced home, focusing on everything but the actual rape. I could not. It hurt too much. Instead, I thought about the faceless Jayce, his kind voice, concerned words, and, most of all, his gentle touch.

I arrived at home, out of breath, wet with sweat, afraid that I reeked of sex, confused by the agony and ecstasy I had just experienced and keenly aware of the inflamed pain I continued to feel.

I'm sure Mom, Dad, and Debbie wondered why I silently took a hot bath and went to bed early on a night as stifling as that one. But no one said a word. My face probably told them not to.

As I soaked in the soothing hot water, I suddenly recalled something Jayce had said. Mick. His name is Mick. No. Rick. Rick! That's what Jayce said. And I know him from somewhere. I tried to concentrate on the glimpse I had had of my assailant's face, not the vicious rape that had occurred. It was easier that way.

But once I turned the lights off in my room and lay tense and alert atop my sheets, the brutal reality of what I had suffered sank in. I began to shiver violently, and despite the sweltering heat, I pulled the linens over myself and curled into a protective embryonic position.

At seventeen, I cried myself to sleep for the last time.

I had an unsettling dream that night, a dream that followed me, haunted me well into my adult years. Over a deserted section of sidewalk a tawdry neon sign flashed *Blow jobs* 9:00 *Tues.* I lay on the concrete, on my back, naked. A faceless man with shoulder-length hair knelt between my spread legs, sucking my cock. One of his hands teased my left nipple, the other softly stroked my right buttock, carefully avoiding touching my asshole without permission. I ran my fingers through his hair. Just as I was about to shoot my load into the phantom cocksucker's mouth, a ghostlike figure wearing a football jersey from my high school appeared leering over his shoulders. I woke up startled, panting, ejaculating a wet dream into a puddle on my abdomen.

I realized immediately why I had recognized the man who had violated so much more than my body. The apparition in my dream was a former football player at my school who had been named all-state lineman during my freshman year, graduated, and then disappeared.

His name was Rick German.

Simply remembering Rick's name offered me some comfort. But it was clear that I could never confront him, not with his overpowering belligerence. I also knew I lacked the courage to tell the police about my rape, as if any man was that strong in the Sixties, so pressing charges against him was out of the question. Besides, the police would say, "You can't prove it. And that's what you get for going into 'the campus can' in the first place! You probably were hoping you'd meet somebody there."

I recognized, then, the one absolute regarding my rape: I could never tell anyone about it. Perhaps they wouldn't believe me. Certainly they wouldn't understand. I could not share this secret with anyone.

Knowing who my rapist was, was frustrating. But not knowing the identity of his accomplice was even more so. Although Jayce had played a key role in my nightmarish experience, I did not think of him with anger or hate. Instead, I was intrigued by him, mysteriously attracted to him. His sympathetic kindness, his calming, yet arousing touch lingered in my mind and libido. I suspected he was as much

Rick's victim as I had been. I needed to find him, to ask him, to know him. And to touch him again.

Perhaps recalling Rick German's name would help me determine Jayce's identity. If I could do that, then maybe I could put the conflicting events of that night behind me.

As fate would have it, I was editor of my high school yearbook. As such, I had access to past annuals and all their photo files. When school began a few weeks after the attack, I took advantage of my position, secretly searching through the archives, studying in detail the books from Rick's junior and senior years, hoping to identify the mysterious Jayce.

I found no one listed in either book with the surname Jayce. What kind of name is that anyway? I asked myself. Is it, in fact, a last name? Could it be a first name? If it were, how many guys named Jayce could there be? I wondered. I found none.

I even scanned the individual pictures in the class sections for Jasons. There were none. I looked closely at all the candid shots in both books, hoping to find one of Rick with a guy with shoulder-length hair. I found none. In fact, Rick's only photos in either book were with the football team. The absence of his junior and, more important, senior pictures indicated to me his antisocial behavior. After all, everyone ordered senior pictures in the Sixties.

About a week into my covert research, I found several envelopes with candid pictures from Rick's senior year that had not been selected for publication. I thumbed through two hurriedly, unsuccessfully. When I pulled out the contents of the final envelope, a photo of Rick glared evilly at me from the top of the stack.

The picture showed Rick and several guys leaning against a '65 Mustang in the school parking lot. In front of Rick, stood a smaller youth with brown, shaggy hair. His face, especially his eyes, grimaced in pain. Rick was wrenching the smaller boy's right arm behind him, twisting it. The glare in Rick's eyes, I realized, was not aimed at me. It reflected a sadistic madman, bullying his smaller victim.

"Do you remember Rick German?" I asked annual staff advisor Paul Feinberg, showing him the picture. Mr. Feinberg not only taught at the school, but had graduated from it. He also served as unofficial alumni historian.

"Sure. All-state football something-or-another," he replied. "Boy, that shot is typical of him. He was a roughneck."

"Who's this guy?" I pumped him further, pointing to the littler youth in the front row.

"That's John Christianson," Mr. Feinberg remembered instantly. "He was sort of a weird guy. Real quiet, timid. Very nice, though. Kind. But he followed Rick everywhere, like a puppy. They called him J.C., like Christ."

"Oh, really," I said dejectedly. "I thought he was someone else."

"Rick called him Jayce. You know, J.C. Jayce. Hear it? It just sort of runs together," Mr. Feinberg added, oblivious to the impact of what he had just told me.

My heart beat like timpani drums. I could feel its pounding in my temples and jugular vein.

"Well, thanks for the info, Mr. Feinberg, but I gotta get home. See you tomorrow," I said calmly, masking my excitement as I put the photos in a safe place in my desk.

All right! I thought to myself as I ran home. Now I know his name. And then I realized the dilemma that faced me. What am I going to do with that information? I challenged myself with uncertainty and trepidation.

Periodically, when no one else was in the yearbook staff room, I would take the photograph from its envelope and study Jayce's face, trying to imagine it without that painful grimace. I had to use my imagination because, like Rick German, Jayce did not pose for a senior picture. Or so I thought. Months later, quite by accident, I found his photograph tacked on at the end of the Senior Section, his name misspelled as Karstenson. I didn't realize it was him at first. Not until I noticed the pain in his eyes.

But, by knowing Jayce's full name, I thought, perhaps, I could contact him. I couldn't, however, find the courage. I hoped I would meet or run into him somewhere, but I did nothing to make that happen. Besides, I feared that if I did see him, Rick would be there, too. So other than hoping for an unexpected rendezvous, I essentially did nothing. And hope, without action, is a useless emotion.

I expected, then, that I would never see Jayce, or Rick for that matter, again.

I endured my senior year, working on the yearbook, scrutinizing the photos from the past when I was alone, reliving my rape in silence, having the recurring neon-blow-job-sign-above-the-sidewalk nightmare, fantasizing about Jayce, and fearing that, somehow, everyone at school knew about my ordeal and what I was thinking.

Because of our yearbook duties, I spent a lot of time with Mr. Feinberg. But I was not comfortable around him.

Paul Feinberg was an odd man. He was about fifty, overweight, and bald, but had an unruly, thick, black beard. He had never married, seemed to have no interests outside of school, and his borderline geekiness was subtly effeminate. He handpicked the editor each year, and the job rarely went to a girl. It was assumed that Paul Feinberg was gay.

In hindsight, I realized he could have been my best ally, strongest supporter, a much-needed mentor. But, instead, because he so repulsed me physically, and because I did not trust him or understand myself, I dealt with him cautiously and aloofly. He was the only other person in my school I thought could possibly have had ideas or experiences similar to mine. Yet I rejected him as a role-model because he represented everything I did not want to be.

I graduated, spent the summer avoiding "the campus can," and entered the University of California at Berkeley to study speech.

That's where I "came out." College, with its freedom from parents and the past, is the time for many people to recognize their homosexuality, and I was one of them. Besides, it was the free-love early Seventies. Having San Francisco nearby certainly did not hurt, either. This time, it appeared, I was in the right place at the right time.

About two years into college, I received a newspaper clipping from my sister. "Local Football Hero Dies in Nam" trumpeted the headline over a thumbnail-size photo of Rick German. The article ended by saying that investigators were looking into the possibility of "friendly fire" causing his death. Debbie scribbled a note in the margin. "Rumor has it that this guy was a real bastard, that his own platoon killed him. Did you know who he was?" she asked innocently.

I smoked a joint alone that night, laughing until I cried. Then I burned the article, dropping its charred remnants into a peace-sign-lined ashtray grave.

My college years were pleasant ones for me. I did well scholastically, enjoyed a busy social life that included both gay and heterosexual people, and participated in more than my share of sex.

Unfortunately, most of the sex was anonymous, occurring in risky places like "the campus can," parks, and bathhouses. Never was it emotionally satisfying. I did not have trouble reaching orgasm in these risky places because I imagined I was with Jayce. But if the sex lost its anonymity, and the Jayce fantasy was replaced with real people, people with names, I could not perform and became depressed.

So, throughout college, I never dated or had sex with a man more than once. As nice, handsome, intelligent, or sexually proficient as they may have been, the men I had sex with never were able to touch me as Jayce had, and I had no reason to go back for seconds, let alone a relationship.

This pattern continued well after college into my late twenties. Gradually I realized that as long as the memory of Jayce limited my feelings and my ability to relate to other men, as long as his touch served as the measure to which all other touch was compared, I would never be able to allow myself to love someone else or enjoy emotionally satisfying sex.

So I wrote to Paul Feinberg, hoping as alumni historian, he would have some news of Jayce.

"All we know about him," he corresponded, "is that he was in the area where Rick German was killed in Vietnam. You did know about that? Anyway, they joined the Marines together, got separated at boot camp, and then, apparently, served near each other over there. After that we have nothing on him."

He's either dead or stateside somewhere, missing in action, I mused.

I had come to the end of the road. I'll never find him, I admitted to myself. It was probably just a fantasy, anyway. And he certainly hasn't been thinking about me for the past ten years. So move on.

I did move on. Finally. It had taken me ten years, ten difficult years, to recover from the pain of Rick's rape and the contradicting pleasure of Jayce's touch. I accepted that, perhaps, God had not intended for me to experience love or emotionally satisfying sex, that he had placed me on earth for another reason. Therefore, I stopped looking for either romance or passion and began practicing celibacy within a generally gay social life.

It was that decision to withdraw, to live an unusual lifestyle within my community, to practice the ultimate method of safe sex, that kept me alive when thousands were dying around me in the holocaust known as the AIDS epidemic.

•__✎

A blur of black and red startled me out of my daydream, as mortarboards sailed ceiling-high and hundreds of graduated seniors whooped, cheered, and hugged below me.

Wow! I exclaimed to myself, feeling sweat on my forehead, I haven't thought about all that in a long time. I wiped my brow with a damp palm. That was really weird, I added, as the audience around me began clapping, calling out individuals by name, waving and rising to their feet.

It was then I realized that my trance had caused me to miss seeing Steven and Brett receive their diplomas. I also realized, at last, why my life had followed the path it had and why I had my need to dialogue with teenagers.

I'm here, as a survivor of the first decade of AIDS, because God wanted me to talk with high school students about decision making and risky behavior, I reflected with a sense of completion. All risky behavior. If there's one thing life has taught me, it is how one decision, one careless choice, can affect a person's life. I finally understood the purpose of my being. As a sense of contentment came over me, the salty sweat drops from my brow dripped into my eyes.

Tears of happiness joined them.

•__✎

Moments later, as the camera-laden onlookers, brimming
with congratulatory messages, merged with the new graduates on the
main floor, I sat anchored alone in my seat, watching the explosion
of hugging below, my tears hidden in a crumpled Kleenex. Finally I
rose slowly and inched my way through the crowd like a late-arriving
party guest.

All I wanted to do was see Steven one final time and leave. I
did not have to talk to him. Not now. Not with tear tracks on my
face. Not after the painful memories and emotional revelation I had
just undergone.

And there he was, with Brett, appropriately, hugging him awkwardly. Their smiles reflected pure pride and joy, as did those of the
people fussing around them. They were family, obviously, especially
the graying man who looked like Steven would in twenty-five years. I
knew I did not belong there. I turned to leave.

"Hey," Steven's voice boomed, as he lunged toward me. "Where
do you think you're going? I want you meet my folks," he requested,
pulling me to them.

When Steven introduced me to the Shepherds as a "really cool
guy," I could tell they had never heard my name before. I had been a
secret from them. Sensitive as he was, Steven knew they may not have
understood our relationship, that they may have become suspicious
or even threatened. I had been one of those friends many children
have who are best kept separate from parents, not because the friendship is bad or wrong, but because it is personal and private.

The Shepherds stepped aside, greeting and congratulating other
students and parents. Steven lightly grabbed my elbow, turning me to
face him. I looked up into his brown eyes, not knowing what he
would say or do next.

"I'll be in touch," he promised. "You know that. Remember, you
gave me permission, Mr. Lerner."

"Tim," I corrected, verbally giving him his graduation present.

Steven swallowed his surprise. "Tim," he repeated, reaching out
with both his arms and pulling me into his firm embrace. I resisted
hugging back. Too many people were watching. Even though this

was graduation, I still had to be careful. I stayed there for several seconds, limply, silently, awkwardly, waiting for him to release me from his arms. He didn't. Finally, I extricated myself from his grasp. Our eyes met.

If I smiled at him, it was briefly, because my upper lip began to quiver, exposing my emotions. I patted him on the back, and, without words, I, embarrassed, turned and disappeared into the dewy, whirling smear of red and black smiles.

• ◞

As the school year ended, I cleaned and organized my office, preparing it for the next year. I marked the proper dates on my calendar for the summer speech therapy workshops I was scheduled to attend. I included visits by my cousin Kate from Los Angeles, my college roommate Mark from Houston, and my friend, David, from back home in Seattle, who I'd known longer than forever. I penciled in tentative dates for trips to Crater Lake, the Columbia River Gorge, Seaside, and Smith Rock. I took a yellow Post-it note and wrote "Get tickets for Shakespeare in Ashland" on it and deliberately stuck it right in the middle of the June page. Another Post-it note with the heading "reading list" was placed at the top of the page. On it I wrote Stephen King, Robert Fulghum, Tom Robbins, and Alice Walker. I even planned to paint the deck of my West Hills condominium and plant some colorful flower boxes for it. That, I hoped, would frame my panoramic view of Portland's skyline with Mt. Hood hovering in the background.

The busier I was, I figured, the less time I would have to think about Steven, what had transpired between us, what was going on in his head, and how he was surviving military life.

I did not expect to hear from him prior to his July 1 departure for boot camp. He had much to do, many friends to see between graduation and his reporting for duty. Surely, I was not a priority. I was surprised, then, to find Steven's voice on my answering machine when I returned home late the night of June 30.

"Hi. This is Steven," the machine echoed. "I was hoping you'd be there so I could say 'good-bye' before I leave in the morning. I'm ready for this, so don't worry about me. OK? And I just wanted to warn you that if your ears burn, buzz, or ring while I'm gone, it's just me talking to you. I'll see you when they let me come home."

I did not hear from him again for more than a month. And, of course, I worried about him. A direct violation of his orders, not to mention my plan for a busy, worry-free summer. But a plain beige postcard did arrive with a short note that simply read, "I'm fine. I could tell you stories!! In fact, I have. Have your ears been tingling since I left?" It was signed Pfc. Steven Shepherd.

• ⤳

The summer passed faster than Carl Lewis in a hurry. September and the new school year arrived, and as the month progressed I realized that boot camp had ended and I had not heard from Steven again. I wondered where he had been sent and how he was doing, although, deep down, I knew he was fine. But I felt lost, somehow, not knowing where he was. This was, I admitted, something over which I had absolutely no control.

By Halloween, I had resigned myself to never hearing from Steven again. To him, I had become merely a pleasant memory from a past lifetime. Our relationship, I feared, would have no closure. I would have no answers. I would go through life never clearly understanding what had or had not happened between us.

I was not angry at Steven for failing to keep in contact with me, although I did feel twinges of disappointment and pangs of resentment when I thought about him. But I understood I had to let go and allow him to move on through his life. He was, after all, only eighteen years old.

New responsibilities at school, more students with speech difficulties, an evening computer class, the yellow Post-it note reading list I had made in June, and my personal social life kept me busy through the fall. But as the chill winds and first flurries of snow heralded

December, the pace slowed down, making time for holiday activities and preparation, most of which I did not particularly enjoy.

Preparation for me meant decorating a small tree with the same gold ornaments, gold beaded chains, and gold lights I had used since the Carter administration. I mailed fewer than twenty cards, not because I had so few friends, but because I had so few friends alive.

By the time winter break arrived, I had finished most of my holiday preparations and was able to sit back, relax, and watch every television holiday special aired. That, I hoped, would improve my attitude and get me into the holiday spirit. But most of the programs, I found, were downright dull. I watched them anyway. Others bordered on pleasant, and a few actually were quite entertaining. However, one, and only one, could be described as "wonderful."

• ➤

It was December 22, 10:00 p.m., and I was watching *It's a Wonderful Life* for the umpteenth time. Just as a tiny bell tinkled inside my television, granting Clarence the Angel his wings, my phone rang unexpectedly.

"This is Steven. I need to talk to you right now," he rattled off like a machine gun.

"Steven?" I shot back in surprise. "Where are you?"

"Down the street at a pay phone. I just got back. My folks don't expect me until tomorrow," he ran on rapidly. "I just walked past your building three times too scared to buzz. Please, Tim, I need to talk," he begged. "Can I come over?"

"I'm here."

In the time it took me to brush my teeth, fill the coffee maker, turn off the TV, and find a soothing radio station that I hoped would help him calm down, Steven reached my buzzer, pressing it insistently.

I let him into the building, opened my door, and waited for him in my entry. I could hear his footsteps coming down the hall, muffled by the carpet, accelerating as they neared my unit.

Steven reached the open door, turned, and faced me, his hair severely short, his shoulders broader than they had been. He dropped his heavy, overpacked duffel bag with a thud at my feet. His face did not react to my smile. Instead it appeared tired, traumatized, and, somehow, dead.

"I killed him!" he blasted at me agitatedly.

"What?" I recoiled in shocked confusion.

"I killed him!" he repeated, angrier, more excited.

My mind raced through the possibilities: A military accident? Military action? But where? And who had he killed? Was it, in fact, military related? Pulling him into the living room toward the couch, I asked, "What are you talking about? Who did you kill, Steven?"

"The baby! I killed the baby!" he confessed painfully.

"What? What are you talking about?" I repeated, more demanding this time. I paused, raised my hands in a "stop" motion, and tried to calm my voice. "Take a deep breath. Start from the beginning. I'm listening," I said as comfortingly as I could considering my confusion.

As I stepped back to sit down, an audible, shivery sigh escaped Steven's lungs.

"During the summer I was fifteen," he began, trembling, "we spent two weeks at Cannon Beach. I met a girl, Allyson, there. The night before we left, she talked me into," he paused and took another deep breath, "having sex with her. She didn't have to pressure me very hard. I was curious. I'd never done it before. Besides no one knew me there. And no one here had to find out. But the weird part, Tim, is that even though I was curious, a part of me really, really did not want to do it. But I did it anyway. I was scared. I didn't know what I was doing, and it was obvious.

"Well, we left the next day," he continued, "but I couldn't forget what I'd done, and I certainly couldn't tell anyone. I just kept thinking about how I failed to be the moral, strong person I was supposed to be. It never dawned on me that Allyson might have gotten pregnant. Hell, Tim, it was only one time, and I did a lousy job," Steven admitted guiltily.

"You had a baby all this time, Steven?" I accused in absolute disbelief. "A baby?"

"No! She had an abortion! An abortion! She aborted my baby!" he screamed. He put his hands to his mouth as if shocked to hear himself saying those words. "She told me about it the following summer when I happened to run into her again at Cannon Beach. She said it so coldly, like it was no big deal. And, damn her, she never even asked me how I felt about it," Steven went on, almost in a trance.

He looked down in shame. I stared straight ahead, speechless. Then, probably subconsciously wanting to postpone having to make a comment, I remembered prepping the coffee maker.

"We need some coffee, Steven. At least I do," I said, avoiding the inevitable. "But don't worry. It's decaf. No high-octane caffeine. Not now," I mumbled distractedly as I rose and went to the kitchen.

Steven was sitting in the same dejected position when I returned with the coffee.

"But, why, Steven, do you feel you killed the baby?" I pressed, cautiously. "You didn't even know Allyson was pregnant. You were totally left out of the decision-making process."

"I know that," he agreed, "but I was the father. I was just as responsible for creating that life. If it weren't for me, the baby would not have been conceived and then killed." With one final reiteration of his exasperation, Steven raised his eyes and focused on my face. "I wasn't even attracted to her."

"Do you know that you were, in fact, the father? Maybe this girl was having sex with other guys," I offered, hoping it would alleviate Steven's guilt and pain. "Just because she told you that you had impregnated . . . "

"I know it was mine, Tim," Steven interrupted tersely. "I just know. In my guts. You see, after she told me, I questioned it, too. So I asked God . . . oh, you're gonna think I'm a flake . . . to help me, to tell me. And he did. No, Tim, God did not speak to me. He just gave me this feeling, this intuition, and I knew. I just knew." Steven paused for a brief moment and then exploded more angrily. "Damn it, Tim. I wasn't raised that way. Stuff like that was not supposed to happen to me. It happens to other guys."

As I sipped my coffee, it all became clear. This baby, this abortion, had been the demon Steven Shepherd had been hiding. This had been what he had wanted to talk to me about all these months. The motive for Steven's running also became clear to me. He was right. He did not run to earn a letterman jacket. Running was what he did to escape from himself and his painful past.

I understood at last. "Steven, you've been keeping this bottled up all these years."

"Yes," he erupted in convulsive sobbing. "I shouldn't have done it!" he added, his tears making him barely understandable.

I reacted instinctively, leaping to the couch, leaning over the distraught young man and hugging him, holding him around the shoulders, pressing his wet face into my chest. His arms were lifeless, limp for a long moment, but I continued to cradle him silently. And while I held him, my mind returned to the revelation I had had months before at graduation. Poor decision-making had greatly affected both our lives, mine at "the campus can," his at Cannon Beach.

I felt movement. Steven was raising his arms, hugging me back, the palms of his hands pressing on my back, pulling me toward him for comfort and support. We remained embraced until his weeping subsided and calm set in. I released him, silently looked into his eyes, gently touched the side of his head, stroking it cautiously, and then returned to my armchair.

"Kid, you've struggled with some heavy shit for a long time," I declared bluntly. "You're going to get through this, though; I'll find a good counselor for you, either here or in the military. The military! Oh, my God! I haven't even had a chance to ask you about army life. Wait! We'll deal with that later," I blathered erratically. He laughed at my spontaneous ranting, his mood rising after the flood of tears had washed the depression, anger, and guilt from his soul.

"But, please, Steven, stop hating yourself for violating your code of morals. Maybe you shouldn't have . . . what the hell . . . fucked Allyson, but you did. And you should have used a condom. But you didn't. You're only human, for God's sake! I think you've learned a lesson here, but I still want you to promise me you will never again have sex with a girl until you are ready and the circumstances are right. In a perfect world, that should be on your honeymoon. But, in the real world, it probably won't." I paused, thinking for only a moment that I was done. "And use condoms, Steven! What the hell were you thinking?"

Steven's brown eyes pierced mine, but he did not answer my question. "You don't get it, do you, Tim? I can't believe this. You still don't get it. I shouldn't have fucked her, not only because it was wrong for me morally, but because it was wrong for me personally, too."

"Personally?" I repeated with a question mark in my voice.

"Being gay and all," he explained matter-of-factly.

My stomach and heart skyrocketed into my throat.

"I knew it even then," he added. "That was going to be the summer when I tried to deal with it, understand it, and accept it."

"And you know I'm gay, too?" I questioned recklessly.

"Well, duh. Of course. I can't believe you're asking me that. I knew you couldn't come right out and tell me back at school. You're a teacher. You'd probably get into major trouble. So I tried to tell you, as subtly as I could, that I knew and that I needed you around. Well, obviously it was too subtle!"

"But I did understand that you wanted me around. I just didn't know why, and because I didn't know why, I wasn't sure if my being gay was even relevant to our friendship. That's why I kept reminding you I was here if you needed me, whatever the reason. This whole situation is so beyond ironic," I chuckled. We chuckled.

"How long have you known that I was gay? Like, what tipped you off?" I inquired. "I don't think I'm obvious."

"No. I don't think anyone else at school knew, if you're worried about that. I never heard anyone gossiping about you," Steven assured me, unaware that, if he was correct, he was fingering himself as my mystery mailman at Columbia. "I knew the day before school started, the day the new teachers were introduced to the faculty. I saw you park your car, and I recognized your pink triangle. See, I'd been reading about the Holocaust that summer, and I'd learned about the symbols the different concentration camp prisoners had to wear. Then, when I threw that football to you at the meeting, and you caught it, I just felt connected to you," he explained with joy. Steven started to chuckle. "Brett actually was assigned to throw to you. I crowded!"

Soothing, calming jazz quietly filled the living room as we stared at each other. "I hope you're feeling better than you did when you got here," I remarked, sensing that he was.

"I am, Tim," he said sincerely. Unexpectedly he rose, came over to my armchair, and gave me a strong hug. "Thank you. A lot. I feel so relieved now that I've told you, told someone."

"Well, thank you for telling me," I countered. "Remember what I said about a counselor," I reminded him as I pulled away from his embrace. "You need a professional to talk to about what happened. We'll find a good one," I promised. But, if you want to talk about being gay, I'm your counselor," I offered. "Now, before we go any further in this conversation, we need to answer some very basic questions, Steven. Are you ready to tackle this?"

"Ready? Tim, I've been waiting for this talk for months."

"OK. How's this for 'basic?' Why do you think you're gay?"

"Why?" he repeated, startled. "Because I'm attracted to guys. Why else? If I told you some of the fantasies I had about guys at school, you'd think I was really twisted."

"Probably not," I disagreed. "But let's not go there. How do you feel about being gay? Are you comfortable with that?"

"Now that I know that's what I am," Steven verbalized without shame. "That's the way I was born. But I used to think, hope, that the 'right' girl would come along and I'd change. But that's not going to happen. I realize that now. Can you tell I've thought about this a lot? I've read a lot about it, too. Anyway, I figured I had to hide it at least until I completed my military duty. But then you came to Columbia with your pink triangle. I watched you park your car, hoping you'd fit my negative expectations. Only, damn you, you caught that fucking football! And my expectations went out the window. Then I met you. I liked you. And I knew then that I had to deal with the reality, the inevitability of my being gay. I couldn't escape it. Through you, somehow, I would have to face it."

Steven paused and sipped the last of his coffee. I took advantage of his momentary silence.

"Wait a minute," I interjected as the empty mug clinked against the glass-topped coffee table. "There's something I don't understand. You're Catholic, right?"

"Yeah."

"Well, the Church certainly hasn't taught you anything positive about homosexuality. Yet you're handling being gay with relative ease. You're defying the Church, you know? You're bucking the system, and that's not like you," I pointed out with a hint of sarcasm. "On the other hand, you support the Church's position on abortion. Don't you see a conflict there?"

"No," Steven defended sharply. "Not at all. The two issues are not even related. Look, I was taught that 'We are all God's children.' Homosexuals, too. I believe He made me this way. I had no choice. And God loves me, accepts me, just as I am. That's all I need to know to accept myself. I can discount, or at least challenge, everything else the Church says regarding homosexuality because none of it is as important as the concepts of God's love and self-love.

"And abortion," Steven continued, raising his voice slightly and pointing his finger at me, "isn't about love at all. It's about murder, choosing murder. It's about killing innocent babies before they have taken their first breath, spoken their first word, taken their first step, or made their first decision. Abortion takes away their freedom of choice, Tim. It takes away their opportunity to reach their fullest potential. It takes away their ability to contribute to or better the world. If a pregnancy must be ended, let God do it. After all, He created the life in the first place."

Steven paused, sighing deeply.

"Anyway," he said, diplomatically returning the conversation to the original question, "before I knew it I had graduated and we had not talked about all this. And then I was at boot camp. Once I got through camp I began to realize that there were other gay people in the army. I could feel it. Their eyes. I got these really strange vibes from some people, and I realized they were 'gay' vibes. I know I can't say anything to any of them or do anything stupid while I'm there, but at least I know I'm not the only one going through this crap."

"Speaking of the army," I jumped in, "why did you enlist in the first place if you knew all along that you were gay?"

"I've already told you why I wanted to join the military. The reasons have not changed," Steven retorted defensively. "And now, I have survived boot camp, learned that I can face any obstacles in my life, and know that I can serve my country well."

"But you'll be doing that in the closet," I pointed out.

"Yes, but I'll be proving them all wrong. I'll be proof that gay soldiers are good soldiers, that gay Americans are good Americans."

"But who's going to know, Steven, if you don't tell them," I yelled, impatient with his lack of logic.

"I'll tell them next year after I get out," he announced. "I just don't know how yet."

"And I'll be with you on that," I supported. "But, you know what? We've gotten way off course here. Now, you've just implied that you've been very cautious on base and that you haven't done anything sexually. Right?"

He nodded affirmatively.

"But have you actually ever had sex with another guy, Steven? I mean, like, that's really basic in determining one's orientation. You don't have to answer that if you feel uncomfortable telling me. I'm only asking because I want you to be sure that you are, in fact, gay and not confused somehow," I explained.

"First of all, I'm not confused. Not anymore. I know I'm gay, Tim. You're not talking me into something. That's what it sounds like. Like you're afraid you'll get blamed for talking me into this. I'm gay. I knew I was gay before I met you," Steven answered, venting his anger at my probing questions. "Second, I feel perfectly comfortable talking to you. For so long, I thought I'd be embarrassed to talk about all of this. But I'm not. Finally I can talk to someone about the real me. Do you know how good that makes me feel, Tim?

"Anyway, yes, I did do it with a guy I met at a track meet last spring," Steven confided. "State finals. His name was Chad. His parents have a huge ranch in Eastern Oregon. He's a rancher, Tim, and he's gay! He was a really nice guy, too, but I think he was even more scared than me. And I was scared! But it felt so right. In my soul, it felt right. It just didn't feel right with Allyson," Steven continued, purging himself of long-held-in tales, thoughts, and feelings.

"Did you use condoms?" I asked seriously.

"We didn't need to. Didn't do that," he explained with a sheepish grin, emphasizing the word "that."

"You probably expect me to ask 'What did you do, then?' but I won't," I said with a twinkle in my eye. "You see," I added more seriously, "there's so much for us to talk about, but we can't possibly cover it all tonight. So, for the moment anyway, let's stick to the basics. However, starting tomorrow any subject is open for discussion. You understand that?"

"Yes, Sir," Steven snapped back. "That's one of the reasons I need you."

"You're right, Soldier," I responded. "Now, here's my final question tonight," I proclaimed. "I just want to be clear on something. Except for that Chad, you've never told anyone else what you're feeling. Right?"

"Never."

"Not even Brett?"

"Especially not Brett," Steven emphasized.

"Why not?"

"Because he won't understand. Remember last fall I told you there are things about me Brett just doesn't understand," he reminded me with dread in his voice. "I'm sure this is one of them."

"How do you know that?"

Steven rolled his eyes skyward. "This is sort of embarrassing. I've never told anyone about this, and I know Brett hasn't either. OK," he hesitated. "We've been best friends since we were five. Real buds. When we were in middle school, we fooled around a few times. OK. The second time, looking and touching wasn't enough for me, and I tried to . . . oh, Jesus, I can't believe I'm saying this to you . . . suck . . . him. I just wanted to do it. Well, he freaked, shoved me away, and said that that was 'really sick.'

"We never did anything again. In fact, he didn't want to have sleepovers or go camping with me after that. I was really confused, hurt, and scared. But he still was my best friend, and I loved him for that. And I think he still liked me, too. But my feelings included fooling around. His did not. And I knew that I could never bring it up again."

"If it will make you feel better," I empathized, "many gay people have similar stories. They share the same pain and the same silence."

"Do you remember when Ms. Nelson died?" he continued. "I told you how she had noticed we were losing our identities. Well, it was me losing mine. I wanted so badly for Brett to stop being afraid of me, to see me the same way he did before I screwed up, that I did everything like him. I dressed like him, I thought like him, and I always agreed with him. Ms. Nelson saw right through my behavior and said that if we were real friends, we would stay friends despite the differences. I think she's wrong about that, though."

"Right or wrong," I said, switching subjects, "it is late. At my house, this is past bedtime." I waited a moment, evaluating all the risks involved and all the scandals that could occur. I ignored them. The emotions and trust that filled the living room told me that it was all right to invite Steven to stay. "I'm assuming that you're crashing here, since your parents aren't expecting you until tomorrow. Do you feel safe sleeping here?"

"Safer than anywhere in the world."

"Good. I think the couch is long enough for you. Is that OK?" I proposed.

"Sure," he said, jumping up and going for the abandoned duffel bag in the hall.

I took a pillow, sheets, and blankets from the hall closet and while I made up the couch, Steven, without an ounce of self-consciousness, stripped to his white briefs behind me. As I crossed the room to silence the jazz emanating from my speakers, Steven crawled into his makeshift bed.

"Do you have any idea what tonight has meant to me, Tim?" he asked, as I turned off the lights.

"Do you have any idea what tonight has meant to me, Steven?" I returned the rhetorical question. "Sleep well, Soldier," I ordered gently as I left the darkened room.

·⤳

I turned the front door dead-bolt and stepped into the bathroom to brush my teeth. I finished and, as I made my way toward my bed, I heard the sounds of Steven's hushed rhythmic breathing whispering to me from the living room. He had already fallen asleep. I peeked down the hall at him, his face airbrushed in moonlight. His peaceful expression, I hoped, reflected the long-awaited serenity he had not felt in years.

I undressed in seconds, climbed into my bed, and shut off the nightstand light. But I lay awake for hours, restless, replaying the evening's conversation, over and over, in my head. I could not silence these echoes until nearly three o'clock, when I finally fell asleep, exhausted. But by then, misty tears of joy had bathed my eyes, overflowing into the crevasses of my deepening crow's feet.

Unfamiliar distant noises interrupted the muted gray stillness of my room when I awoke late the next morning. I leaped from my bed, sprung into the hall, and spun toward the gurgling noises coming from the kitchen. Steven was preparing coffee, wearing only white briefs and a gold crucifix, which dangled from his neck.

"Hi," he chirped. "I hope you slept as well as I did."

"I slept well, once I got to sleep," I affirmed groggily, as I tripped toward the stereo and turned it on, locating a station I thought Steven would enjoy. I returned to the kitchen and prepared a plate of bagels, butter, and grape jelly.

"Before we continue our conversation from last night, I have a question I have to ask you," Steven led off, watching the coffee machine. "Last night, you did all the asking. Now it's my turn, and I've needed to know this for a long time. There's no easy way to ask this." Then he stopped, faced me, and timidly asked, "Tim, do you have AIDS?"

"No. I'm fine. I don't even have the virus," I told him as his face went from concerned to comforted.

"Good. I'm glad. Thank you, God," Steven expressed with relief. "I've always been afraid that you would die before I got up the guts to talk to you."

"I'm not going to die on you," I assured him. "Now you promise me the same thing."

"I'm going to have Willard Scott announce my hundredth birthday on *The Today Show*," he joked, masking his promise in humor, "if he's still alive."

The coffee machine finished burbling, and we took our caffeine-filled mugs into the living room. For nearly two hours we talked about AIDS, safer sex practices, appropriate ways to meet other gay people, homosexuality in the military, schoolmates to whom he'd been attracted, and his life since I had last seen him. And we drank coffee. Lots of coffee.

As our conversation wound down, we decided that since Steven's family did not know when to expect him, as he allegedly was flying standby, I would drop him off near his home. I suggested it was time to start the showering procedure and found him a towel. While he showered, I made my bed and turned his "bed" into a couch again.

This is absolutely unbelievable, I told myself, as I plopped into my armchair and waited for my unexpected guest to step from the steamy bathroom.

Steven took a long shower, probably because he had been denied the time, freedom, privacy, and luxury to do so for months. When he finally emerged through the door, wrapped in the damp towel, he looked as contented as ever I'd seen him. But I had little time to appreciate the vision.

"It's your turn," he announced.

I showered, shaved, and dressed in less than twenty minutes, and when I was done, Steven was waiting for me on the couch wearing top-siders, navy blue slacks, and a white button-down-collar shirt with blue pin stripes.

"After all you've been through since last June, after all we've gone through, after all we've talked about," I sarcastically noted, "look at you. Nothing's changed. You're still the same preppie punk you were when I first met you!"

"Yeah, but now I'm a gay preppie punk," he crowed.

"All right!" I celebrated, as we high-fived.

"Well, are we ready to go?" I asked.

"Not yet. I want to ask you one more thing, Tim. Something I don't understand," Steven requested hesitantly.

"Sure."

"Why didn't you want me in your bed?" he asked with hurt in his voice. "I thought we were supposed to do something last night. What did I do wrong?"

"Nothing. Nothing," I repeated, startled by his feeling rejected. "You didn't do anything wrong. Is that bothering you? God, I'm sorry if it is," I apologized, "but just because we're both gay doesn't mean we have to have sex, Steven. I'm old enough to be your father. Don't you think that would have been weird? I do."

"Yeah, I guess it would have been weird. I just thought . . . " he trailed off with a puzzled look on his face. "No offense," he offered as appeasement.

"You just don't go around having sex with every gay man you meet just because they're gay," I continued, with what was becoming a lecture. "There are people out there who would like you to believe that gay men do nothing more than have sex with each other. They've been spreading that lie, that stereotype, for decades. There's got to be some kind of physical and, more importantly, mental attraction between the two guys. And you know what? Even when you have that, you're not required to have sex either. You're allowed to set your own guidelines. Being gay is not just about sex, Steven. But you'll learn about that. Now, come on. Let's go. It's time for you to see Mom and Dad," I urged as we rose together.

"Tim?" he said tentatively. "You know I love you, anyway."

"If you don't know how much I love you, Steven, you must be the stupidest, blindest, most insensitive man ever to walk the earth. But our relationship can't be about sex. It's about something more special than that."

Steven reached over, gently cupped my shoulders in his hands, and lightly kissed my forehead. He picked up his khaki bag, and we left the safe protection of my condo and entered the real world, the cruel world.

• ⬎

The air was chilly and the sky clear, exposing a vibrant white Mt. Hood in the distance as we drove across Portland to Steven's home. He told me of his holiday plans in excited tones that probably exposed his happiness at being home again more than he intended. He would spend time with his family through Christmas Day. Then, if Brett were home for the holiday break from the University of Oregon, he would spend the next day with him. That was a tradition. That day had always been set aside for their early-morning gift exchange, which was followed by going together to return presents that were the wrong size, the wrong color, or the wrong idea. Finally, between December 27 and December 30, Steven would be in San Francisco reuniting with cousins from Indiana whom he had not seen since childhood.

"But I will call you when I get back," he swore. He would return to army life in Germany on January 3.

"I'll be in town the entire vacation," I remarked with resignation in my voice. "Christmas will be at my sister's house as usual. She's lived here for about five years now. Her husband, Ted, and their kids, Adam and Sarah, will be there, as will her mother-in-law and our folks, who will be driving down from Seattle."

I pulled the car into an empty, but littered, convenience store parking lot near the Shepherd home at Steven's urging. "Have a good Christmas, Soldier," I wished. "Enjoy San Francisco. But don't leave your heart there. And call me when you get back. I'll want a report on how things went with Brett."

"I will," he answered as he got out of the car. "Thanks for everything. You've given me the best Christmas present I could possibly get. Merry Merry!"

As Steven walked toward the residential street at the end of the parking lot, a red Honda CRX nosed up to the store. Out jumped a clean-cut, conservative-looking blond young man wearing an Oregon State sweatshirt. His eyes followed Steven as he trudged away, lugging the heavy khaki bag.

The OSU man tripped on the curb in front of the store and then refocused his attention on his mission.

It was then I noticed the pink triangle in the corner of the CRX's rear window. "Oh, my God," I remembered, "I haven't asked Steven about the paper pink triangles!"

"Steven," I called as I pulled up to him in the lot's side street entrance, "did you ever put anything in my mailbox back at school?"

"No. Why?" he asked, puzzled, eliminating himself as my mystery confidant.

"Nothing. Never mind. Have fun," I said minimizing my confusion as I drove off. Through my rear-view mirror I noticed again the parked crimson CRX with its pink triangle. Its bold vanity plate read "CHAD."

•➤

I was not surprised when Steven called me early New Year's Eve. We exchanged small talk about our holiday activities and his experiences in California with his relatives. New Year's Eve would be spent with his parents, he announced without complaining.

"I'm getting ready to party with a bunch of friends until, oh, 1991," I revealed. "But enough of this chitchat," I snarled, impatiently. "How was your day with Brett?"

"I thought you'd never ask," Steven rebounded. "It was weird, very weird. He's changed, Tim. And I don't know how or why. But he's changed."

"What do you mean 'changed?'" I pried.

"Well, first of all, you wouldn't recognize him. His hair is short, clean, and kind of like mine when I was a civilian. And he's dressing very, you won't believe this, nice. And he's been working out! Brett Weiss has been lifting weights. He's got muscles, Tim."

"Did you ask him why the change?" I pursued.

"Yes. But he was real vague, mysterious. He was distant, somehow, like he didn't want to talk about it, like it was a secret or something. God, I hope he's not in some kind of trouble."

"Oh, I doubt it. But was it awkward seeing him again?" I asked.

"Definitely. But we did have fun. He really likes U of O and says he's got friends there," Steven relayed. "But he didn't talk about them either."

"Did you tell him that you're gay?" I asked directly.

"Hell no! Even if I wanted to tell him, I couldn't have because he was so distant and evasive. I really don't understand him. Maybe we are just growing apart, going in different directions," he theorized.

"Maybe . . . "

•➤

My mother's New Year's Day call came too early. I was up, but I hadn't slept enough. And I was hung-over. I was drinking my second cup of coffee, watching the Pasadena Rose Parade on TV, and thinking how the motion of the floats was making me nauseous.

"Yes, Mom, I'll have a good year," I said, obediently. "And I'll promise to stay healthy if you promise not to sing 'Auld Lang Syne.'"

She promised.

"I have something else to talk to you about," she said, changing the subject. "Do you remember Ross Lindstrom? Wasn't he the baseball coach when you were in high school?"

"Yeah. Why?"

"He was that really handsome one, right? The one that turned down a professional baseball contract to teach social studies and coach high school ball?" Mom said, continuing her grilling.

"Where are you going with this, Mother?" I barked with irritation.

"Well, I think I know why. He died of AIDS on Christmas, Timmy," she answered, stunning me. "I read it in the *Times*. He was gay. He probably didn't think there was a place for him in pro sports, under the spotlight, in the public eye and all. Apparently, he felt safer, even as a closeted teacher, here. What a tragedy! He gave up his dream, without testing his talent. And then to die like this. How sad!" She paused, waiting for me to respond.

I was speechless.

"And what a waste!" she added.

"Waste?" I blurted in anger. "Ross Lindstrom was a good coach, Mom. The man knew his baseball. And he knew world history. He was a terrific teacher. Remember how much I loved his class? A waste,

Mom? Look how many kids benefited from knowing him as a teacher or coach. I did."

And then I realized how much more I could have gained from him had it been a different time, had he been allowed to be openly gay. Ross Lindstrom could have been the ally, role-model, mentor, and friend I had desperately needed in school, the one I had not allowed Paul Feinberg to be.

"Thanks for letting me know, Mom. But I've got to go. I think I'm going to lose it," I mumbled in a cracking voice as I weakly hung up the phone.

And I did.

Steven returned to the army in early January and served the entire balance of his military career in Germany, missing out on the disruption and inconvenience of frequent relocations that many soldiers experience. Miraculously, his unit was not sent to the Middle East during Operation Desert Storm, but stayed in Germany processing soldiers as they passed through on their way back to the States.

He sent me several postcards during that year and a half, always mentioning his good health and spirits, but cautiously saying little else. He had been, I later found out, maintaining similar communication with Brett.

By the time Steven received his discharge in July 1992 and returned to Portland, he had been accepted at the University of Oregon in Eugene to begin courses that fall. History would be his major. He had selected the U of O because of its proximity to home, its serene tree-filled campus, and its tradition as a track and field power.

Besides, Brett, his longtime friend, would be there. Even if their relationship seemed strained, it would be helpful, Steven felt, to have someone he knew nearby. However, Brett, who lived in Eugene year-round, received the news of Steven's enrollment icily, aloofly, which widened the growing gap between them. Although the boys lived less than an hour and a half apart that summer, they saw each other only once when Brett briefly visited Portland.

Steven and I, though, saw quite a lot of each other. He called me the day after he returned home, talking nonstop through three sit-com reruns, recounting his experiences in Germany. None, he pointed out, were sexual.

"But I thought a lot about Allyson and the baby, Tim. And I'm still having a real hard time dealing with the abortion," he admitted. "I don't know what would have been the right answer. But I know that wasn't it. I know I couldn't have raised the baby then. I couldn't have even helped pay Allyson's medical expenses if she had had the baby and we had put it up for adoption," Steven said, analyzing the haunting situation yet another time, searching for an answer. "But if she had discussed it with me, maybe we would have come up with something, anything, and I wouldn't still be so damn pissed off."

"Have you talked to anyone about this? Weren't there any military psychiatrists in Germany?" I asked.

"I wouldn't talk to a military shrink about anything."

"Well, then we'll find someone here. I think I promised you that before you left for Germany," I remembered. "I know the right guy. I'll call him tomorrow."

Raleigh Davidson was a psychiatrist I had known for several years through the gym to which I belonged. He was a Southern transplant, from Atlanta. His drawl was as comforting as iced tea on a shady verandah in August, and Southern charm oozed from him like nectar dripping from an overripe peach. He was fortyish, partnered with Geoff for a dozen years, and in better shape than was necessary for a man no longer on the hunt. He specialized in self-esteem issues and anger management.

Raleigh talked with Steven three or four times during July and August, focusing on his anger at Allyson for not including him in the abortion decision. I'd asked Raleigh to try to limit the counseling to that, if possible, avoiding issues regarding sexual orientation. That is my territory, I told him, even if I am not a professional. Besides, Steven seemed to be fine regarding his orientation. Raleigh respected my relationship with Steven, understood my concerns, and honored my conditions.

Their sessions quickly helped Steven see that he needed to confront Allyson to purge himself of his anger. He needed to ask her the questions he'd been asking himself since Cannon Beach. However, since he was unable to locate her, Steven had to settle for a series of mock confrontations in which he faced an imagined Allyson and vented his wrath.

By the end of August, Steven had gone through this exercise three times. Once with Raleigh. Once with me. And once alone. Steven had almost purged himself of the poisonous anger within him. Almost.

• ➤

I didn't see Steven again before he moved to Eugene, but he called me regularly on the phone.

Our frequent conversations, it seemed, brought us even closer than we had been. Perhaps because he was facing the unknowns of college life, Steven needed my friendship now more as a security blanket than as an "ear or shoulder." His motivation, though, was unimportant to me, for I enjoyed every phone call, every detailed phone call, because they enabled me to continue being included in Steven's life, witnessing its conversations, experiences, and events even though we were miles apart.

The first important event Steven reported to me occurred the first weekend of September. The annual Shepherd Family Labor Day Picnic was a tradition etched in charcoal briquettes. It marked the end of summer and meant the beginning of a new school year. Attendance was required. Absences were excused only if one were either exploring another planet or in the army. So, Steven had not participated since 1989.

He had missed the barbecue smells, the joyful sounds, the warm feelings of the picnic greatly, and he eagerly looked forward to being part of it again. But he also felt trepidation as the holiday approached, for Steven had decided it would be over the three-day weekend, before he began college, that he would "come out" to his parents, telling them of his sexuality and fleeing the darkest closet of them all, the familial one.

Mrs. Shepherd spent Labor Day scurrying around in a frenzied, yet organized, manner preparing for the guests who were to arrive around four o'clock. Steven's sister, Crystal, who at twenty-three resented still being expected to participate, begrudgingly assisted.

The guests could be as few as two or three familiar people or as many as twelve total strangers, as they had been a few years before when two recently immigrated Russian Jewish families were invited. The guest list always was decided by Mrs. Shepherd, and it was a secret she protected with determination. This, too, was part of the tradition. So, when Mr. and Mrs. Weiss, Brett's parents, arrived with a homemade apple pie and a cookie tin full of lemon bars, Steven was quite surprised.

"Where's Brett?" Mrs. Shepherd called from the kitchen as Steven greeted Mrs. Weiss in the doorway, hugging her. Mr. Weiss saluted Steven militarily and then patted him on the shoulder as he passed, heading to the kitchen to deliver the aromatic desserts.

"Brett's staying in Eugene this weekend as usual. I couldn't talk him into coming home, even for this," Mrs. Weiss explained, disappointing both Steven and his mother, who had intended the picnic to bring the boys closer together again. "He says 'Hi' and that he'll see Steven in Eugene in a few days."

"Sure," Steven agreed with faked cheerfulness, silently wondering why his friend continued to show so little interest in maintaining their friendship.

The Weisses immediately began asking about Steven's military experiences, causing Crystal, who had heard her brother's tales too many times, to retreat to the silent front porch. At first, Steven genuinely enjoyed telling his tales. But, why, he thought, isn't Brett here asking these questions? I should be telling him these stories.

However, as the conversation continued, often lapsing into irrelevant small talk, and the barbecue began blowing hickory-scented clouds across the back yard, Steven became increasingly distracted, aware of the potentially explosive situation looming ahead. As soon as they leave, I have to tell Mom and Dad, he reminded himself.

By the time the burgers had been cooked to the specifications of all present, Steven had worked himself into quite a nervous state, meandering about aimlessly, unable to focus on the conversations around him. He carelessly spread lettuce, mayonnaise, catsup, and rel-

ish on a puffy, plain hamburger bun, scooped a dollop of the traditional mustard and bacon-flavored potato salad on his paper plate,
and inconspicuously escaped to his room to eat his holiday feast
alone, wallowing in his secret anxiety.

He did not return to the smoky back yard until Mrs. Weiss began
slicing her fragrant, fresh dessert more than half an hour later.

"What are Brett's housemates like?" he asked her as she handed
him a paper plate sagging with an ample piece of apple pie.

"They're really nice boys, Steven," she answered, placing a lemon
bar next to the pie on his plate. "You haven't met them yet, have you?
They don't come up to Portland often. In fact, Brett doesn't even
come home very much anymore," she added with a tinge of sadness
in her voice. "They all seem to be perfectly content in Eugene. But
they're nice boys. I'm sure you will like them."

Steven scanned the yard. "Hey, where's Crystal?" he asked, noticing her absence.

"She left right after dinner. Said she was going to have dessert with
friends in Beaverton," Mrs. Weiss whispered. "But don't mention it to
your mother. She is not pleased."

Mr. and Mrs. Weiss left an hour later, laden with the cookie tin,
still half full of lemon bars, and a Tupperware container stuffed with
potato salad. As the sounds of their departing car faded in the distance, Mr. Shepherd plopped into his beige recliner, undid his belt,
and reached for the newspaper lying on the table next to the chair.

"Before you start reading the paper, Dad, I need to talk to you
about something," Steven announced with a dry mouth, as the hamburger, potato salad, pie, and lemon bar began to petrify in his stomach. "You, too, Mom. 'Cause if I don't do it now, I don't know when
I'll get another chance, with my going away and everything."

"What is it, Steven?" Mrs. Shepherd said with a mix of curiosity,
fatigue, and irritation. "I really should clean up before I go to bed."

"I'll clean up, Mom. I always did before, didn't I?" Steven reminded her.

"Yes, you did. Oh, why can't Crystal be more like you?" Mrs.
Shepherd wished aloud.

With his mother appearing both tired and angry, Steven feared
that perhaps he had picked a potentially disastrous time for this
important conversation. But he knew he could not turn back. It was

now or never. Cautiously, then, he reached through the darkness of the closet, carefully grabbing the door knob. He began turning it.

"Have you heard from Lynne Burgess recently?" Steven inquired, preparing his parents for his revelation.

"Lynne? No, not for, oh, two years now," Mrs. Shepherd answered slowly. "I'm sure she just got tired of getting the cold-shoulder from Crystal. Gosh, I was so disappointed in your sister, treating Lynne so poorly after she got that letter. But why are you asking about Lynne? Have you seen her? Is she OK?"

"No, I haven't seen her. I've just thought about her a lot the past few months. Missing her. Mom, do you remember what you said when Crystal showed you that letter?" Steven asked, anticipating a negative response.

"Yes, I do. Something about all of us being God's children, I think," responded Mrs. Shepherd, surprising her son.

"Yeah, you did, Mom. Why'd you say that?"

"Because we all are God's children. You see, maybe a week before your sister got Lynne's letter, I was watching Oprah," explained Mrs. Shepherd, pulling details of the program from the recesses of her memory. "There was this woman whose daughter had recently committed suicide. The girl had just told her parents that she was a lesbian, and they threw her out of the house. The woman was beside herself in grief, blaming herself for the girl's death. She said she had not known any other way to react to being told that she had a lesbian daughter. She knew nothing about the subject, had never considered it, wasn't prepared for it, and couldn't accept it. But her daughter's suicide made her realize that she had been wrong.

"'If we are God's children, as we've been taught,' she repented, 'then God created us all and accepts us as we are. Even lesbians and homosexual men. If He can do that,' the woman said, 'so can we.' So when Crystal showed me Lynne's letter, I remembered that woman's sobbing face and her very real reminder that we all are, indeed, God's children."

"Do you still believe that, Mom?"

"Well, of course I do. I guess I just failed to instill that lesson in Crystal," she answered remorsefully. "She's probably lost a good friend. Your sister can be so stubborn sometimes."

Mr. Shepherd, who had remained silent, observing the mother–son conversation like a spectator at a tennis match, shifted in his chair. "Why are we talking about this, Steven?" he asked suspiciously.

Steven paused. He looked directly at his father.

"Because I might be gay, too."

"What?!" his father shot back in surprise.

"Because I am gay, too," Steven corrected, unintimidated by his father's reaction.

"Jesus Christ. Are you sure?" Mr. Shepherd asked after a moment of deafening silence.

"Yes."

"No, Steven. This is just a phase. You're just feeling lonely because you've been home two months now and haven't met the right girl," Mrs. Shepherd jumped in.

"It's not a phase, Mom. And I'm not looking for the right girl."

"Well, then, how long have you felt this way?"

"A long time. A long, long time. But right now I just need to know if you can deal with it. Both of you."

"Deal with it?" repeated Steven's perplexed father. "No! Yes. I have to, I guess. I don't have a choice, now do I? You're my son. Just give me some time, though. Please."

Suddenly, Mrs. Shepherd gasped. "Oh, my God, Steven!"

Steven looked up, startled. "What is it?"

"Do you know what that poor girl's name was? Stevie, her name was Stevie! The girl who killed herself. Her name was Stevie," Mrs. Shepherd said as she erupted in nervous laughter.

"Stevie? Like you used to call me?" he clarified, catching the irony that had triggered his mother's reaction. Laughter, tension-freeing laughter, exploded from Steven's smile, growing rapidly louder. Tears began rolling down his cheeks.

"Stevie!" Mrs. Shepherd spat out again incoherently, as her laughter became out-of-control, nearing the level of hysteria.

As he wiped his cheeks, Steven stepped to his mother's side, reaching out to embrace her.

"Stevie!" she reiterated convulsively a third time, as she fell into her son's arms, weakly pounding him on the back.

Mr. Shepherd watched his wife's and son's uncharacteristic outburst with no reaction. He seemed isolated, alone, peering past them, deep in thought. "Deal with it," he mumbled to himself as he began to shift back in his recliner.

"Oh, damn," he exploded abruptly. "I've got pie filling all over my pants. Why didn't someone tell me that?" he barked.

• ⤍

Steven's move to Eugene in the fall did not end our frequent telephone talks. Except for his irregular visits to Portland, and my even rarer trips to Eugene, the phone was how we maintained communication, and how I learned about college life Steven-style.

Steven settled in a well-maintained Victorian boardinghouse near the U of O campus, arriving on a muggy, overcast day. Brett met him there and helped him unload from Steven's recently purchased dark-blue Chevy pickup the few boxes of books and kitchen supplies, Steven's rarely used accordion, and the suitcases stuffed with Ivy League duds. His face, however, continued to reflect the cool, cordial distance Steven had grown to resent so much. Only now a new nervousness had been added.

After the TV and stereo had been removed from the cab of the truck and deposited into the fresh paint–scented room, Steven asked Brett if they could go to his house for a tour.

"I'd like to meet your housemates finally. You never talk about them," he said innocently.

"Can't do that. They're not home. Besides, you won't like them," Brett curtly answered, rejecting the request.

Steven exploded. "What the fuck is going on here, Brett? You act like I'm intruding in your world. You've acted like that since you moved here. I just need a friend. I don't know anybody here!"

"You need to find other friends, Steven," Brett advised calmly.

"Why?" Steven demanded. "Are you guys running a drug lab or in a cult or something?" he half-seriously charged. "Shit! I don't know you anymore, Brett!"

"No, you don't," he agreed, turning his back on Steven, evasively looking out the window. "My friends are . . . gay. We're gay. I'm gay. There. I said it. Now, do you understand?"

Steven Shepherd's jaw went limp. His mind raced, tracing the entire course of his friendship with Brett. Screeching to a halt, his mind focused on the middle school years, the sexual rebuff, Ms. Nelson's talk, and the distance that had grown between them.

Oh, my God, he thought, instantaneously comprehending all that had happened during the past seven years. He now understood why Brett had been acting as he had. Brett had never rejected him. Denial, confusion, and guilt had caused Brett to reject himself. He then escaped from himself by adopting a heavy metal image, just like Steven had done when he began running. And now he thinks I'm going to freak out on him, Steven assessed, realizing the irony. Hell, he's been going through as much confusion, pain, and searching as I have. Maybe more.

His mind spinning in a whirlwind of joy and relief, Steven stepped forward, stopping directly in back of Brett. He looked out the window, over Brett's shoulder.

"I understand perfectly," he whispered as a mist enveloped Eugene, blurring his view. He slid his arms around Brett's torso—hugging him, pulling him into his embrace—and lovingly kissed Brett on the nape of the neck.

•　⟿

When I returned home from school that day I found my
answering machine's red light blinking urgently. I pressed the "play"
button and heard an unexpected voice.

"Tim. It's Steven," the recorder regurgitated. "God, I wish you were
home already. You won't believe what I have to tell you. Call me
A.S.A.P. I said 'A.S.A.P.!'" Then he left his new number.

I frantically began dialing the number before the message had
completely rewound. Shit! What could be the matter? What could be
so urgent that it demanded two A.S.A.P.'s? I wondered.

The telephone was picked up on the first ring. "Hello," Steven
answered breathlessly.

"What's the matter? Are you OK?" I asked anxiously.

"Tim. Tim. Tim," Steven repeated, in an excited staccato. "You will
never guess where I am right now."

"Eugene," I responded, noting the obvious.

"More specific!"

"Your new room. That boardinghouse."

"More specific, Tim."

"More specific?" I repeated. "Well, your voice, no, your breathing
sounds weird, sort of out of breath. You're not running, are you? Are
you on a cell-phone?"

"Cell-phone? No. He thinks I'm running," he seemed to relay to
someone else. "I'm in bed, Tim. Now guess who's with me," Steven
ordered from the cluttered cardboard and canvas jungle of stacked
boxes, bags, and suitcases in his room.

"I don't know, Steven. How would I even . . . " I responded, obviously perturbed by the direction in which this game had gone.

"Brett!"

"Brett?" I uttered in amazement.

"Yes. He's gay, Tim. Brett's gay. I'm gay. You're gay. We're all a
bunch of queers!" Steven exploded in laughter. Immediately a second
out-of-control hysterical cackling erupted in the background. For two,
three, maybe four minutes, I listened to the combined shrieks of their
joyous jubilation.

"Hi, Mr. Lerner. It's me," Brett attempted to say into the phone before the next outburst escaped.

Then Steven tried to talk again. But more giggles gagged him, making his sputtered utterings, at best, vaguely understandable. "Choctaw 'gator paws, head to tail, you know," he garbled. Then he hung up.

It took me quite a while to decipher what he had said. It was "Talk to you later. Call. Hadda tell you now."

• ➤

My brief, bizarre telephone conversation with Steven and Brett so flabbergasted me that I found it impossible to concentrate at work the next day. I was overwhelmingly giddy with emotion, a mental state foreign to me. On several occasions during the day, I began to laugh uncontrollably. One attack occurred while Lucia Santarosa, a recent El Salvadoran immigrant sat expressionless at my desk. Hysteria, or at least some form of hysteria, perhaps, had been a common response to the atrocities in her homeland. My fit of cackling apparently was nothing unusual to her and demanded no explanation. She showed no visible reaction.

As Lucia left, I closed my office door. If I lost it again, I would do so without witnesses. And luckily, Lucia had been the only scheduled one-on-one for the day.

This day had been planned as a catch-up day. Way behind in reports and assessments, I tried to concentrate on them, but my mind kept flashing on bits of past conversations with Steven, tracing the course his and Brett's friendship had run, and watching the hands of my office wall clock slowly plod onward, like an aimless window-shopper meandering through a mall.

Periodically, I would giggle, pace restlessly, and then giggle some more. My motivation to get through this odd, eternal day was the assumption that Steven would call me that evening with an apology and an explanation.

My prediction was right. Steven called just as *Seinfeld* began, just as Kramer semi-slipped, semi-tripped into Jerry's living room. And mine.

"Yes, Operator, I will accept a call from Eugene, Oregon," I intuitively answered, abandoning the traditional "Hello."

"How'd you know it was me?" Steven asked, startled by the unorthodox greeting.

"Well, it had better be you! Talk to me."

"Can you believe this, Tim? This is so strange," Steven said, beginning his nonstop, rapid raving. "God, I don't know where to begin. I'm so unfocused. I can't concentrate. I thought running and the army taught me how to focus! I've got to get my shit together. Classes begin in a week and a half. Anyway, how'd all this happen? OK. I sorta confronted Brett about the way he'd been acting, so distant and all, and he just blurted out that he and his friends were gay and I just grabbed him and hugged him and whispered 'Me, too,' and then we like . . . started crying.

"After a few minutes, he told me that, for years, he'd been afraid that I would reject him, dump our friendship, if I found out. So he purposely tried to push me away, so he wouldn't have to tell me. Does any of this make any sense?"

"Yes. What happened next?" I urged.

"Well, we just stood there at the window, looking toward the campus, and he apologized for overreacting, freaking out, back in middle school when we were fooling around. He'd always known he blew it . . . no pun intended . . . sorry for the terrible pun, Tim . . . but he was confused, didn't understand his own feelings, and thought I was just going through a phase, acting silly or something, because I couldn't have been gay, too, since I was planning to join the army.

"God, I'm just rambling, Tim. Am I making any sense? Anyway, then he told me that a few days after the incident, he realized he really did want to do it, too . . . and get this . . . that he was in love with me. But he didn't know how to go back and fix what had happened. And besides, he thought, that since I couldn't be gay, I wasn't feeling what he was feeling anyway. So, for like seven years, Brett and I just avoided the whole thing, playing this fucked-up game."

"And you both struggled and suffered alone in silence," I added sadly.

"Yeah. But that's in the past," Steven philosophized, his voice trailing off in thought. "At some point, while we were talking at the window, he asked if it were OK if he were still in love with me. Well, I answered by pulling him to the floor under the window sill and . . . we did it, finally . . . right there next to all my unopened boxes and crap.

"And when we were done, we realized we were lying in front of the open closet door. Isn't that a hoot?" Steven confided, chuckling. "Then we got up, made my bed, got in it, and that's when we called you."

"I'm really glad for you, Steven. I mean I'm really glad for you. And Brett," I gushed.

"Man, am I happy. And relieved. I've never felt like this, Tim. I think I'm in love. No. I know I'm in love. We're in love. This is so cool, so fuckin' cool. I just don't know why we had to wait so long to figure it all out," Steven wondered aloud.

"Maybe because God thinks you can handle it now," I theorized. "They say the Lord works in mysterious ways. Now, I have two questions, really important ones, to ask."

"OK. Shoot," Steven shot back.

"Which china pattern have you selected? And where are you registered?" I teased.

•◢

Two weeks later, I sent Steven a good luck gift to celebrate the beginning of his college career. It was a book, a small one, my worn, torn, tattered copy of *The Official Preppy Handbook*, a satire of preppie values and lives published in the early 1980s.

"I finally figured out why you really chose to be a U of O Duck. Yeah, it had something to do with Brett. Yeah, it's close to home. OK. The track and field tradition played a part in your decision," I wrote sarcastically. "But the real reason you're there is the Ducks, you preppie punk! Ducks are very preppie, you know. Check out page twenty-three, 'The Duck Motif.'"

Several evenings later, as I was watching MTV, and wondering why, Steven called.

"Duck you!" he attacked caustically.

"Hey, Mallard Mouth," I responded, sticking with the duck theme. "How is the college man?"

"Things are great here," he reported. "My classes are interesting, harder than I imagined. There's a lot more studying required than in high school. But I'll do fine."

Steven said he and Brett were spending as much time together as their schedules allowed. In addition to school, Brett was working part-time in the school's main library, while Steven had begun running on a daily basis again.

Brett's housemates, who had heard his endless tales about Steven for nearly two years, accepted the new collegian as part of the house-hold immediately, and he slept at their place regularly. Everyone agreed to put off any changes in official living arrangements until the end of December's holiday break. Steven would then move into the house to start off the new year.

From the moment Steven met Brett's housemates, Joe Mangini and Damon Whitaker, he liked them. He could see how the similarities and common bonds they all shared could lead to great camaraderie.

Joe had been senior class president at a Catholic school in sub-urban West Portland. He was quiet, studious, an organizer, and the domestic housemate, always picking up after the others. Joe was a talented tennis player who would play whenever he could. He even enjoyed teaching novices who showed an interest in learning the game.

Damon Whitaker was everything Joe wasn't. He was brash, impulsive, and, except for his personal appearance, a slob. He came from Bend, Oregon, where he, like Steven, had been his school's student body president. Because Bend is at the base of the state's best ski slopes, Damon had become an excellent recreational skier. But his most prominent traits were his wry sense of humor and con-tagious smile.

"I like you already," he told Steven when Brett introduced them.

"Why?" Steven rebutted cautiously. "You don't know me yet."

"You're a homo, aren't you?" Damon teased, his grin announcing his playfulness.

Brett had met Damon first, during freshman orientation. They had clicked immediately, sensing an unspoken connection. They came out together at their dorm's Halloween party, where they appeared to have a bit too much fun dressed as, and mocking, the irritatingly peppy U of O cheerleaders. As they decostumed in Damon's room after the party, their conversation evolved from silly cheerleader chatter to serious self-evaluation. Three hours later, Brett and Damon determined that the unspoken connection that had brought them together was an immediate shared attraction for a blond junior on the fourth floor named Josh, who they had learned quickly was not attracted to them but to every female between eighteen and twenty-five in or near Eugene.

Together, Brett and Damon met Joe at the November Gay and Lesbian Association of Ducks (GLAD) meeting. It had been Damon's idea to attend.

"I need to meet other gay people on campus, and I'm not going alone. You have to go with me," he ordered Brett. "I want to see who belongs and what they do."

Joe went to that meeting, too, alone and nervous. It was the first time he had acted on his secret feelings of homosexuality. Damon saw him timidly pacing in front of the open meeting room door and recognized him from their Economics 101 lecture section.

"I would have never guessed that you're gay," a smiling Damon told him when he finally entered the classroom-turned-meeting room.

"I'm not sure I am. I guess I'm here to find out. This is my first meeting," Joe waffled.

"If you're here and you're as nervous as you look, you're gay," Damon postulated. "This is our first meeting, too. I guess that makes us all virgins. I'm Damon, and this is Brett," he said, offering a firm handshake.

"Joe."

"I'm just as scared as you are, Joe," Damon said, trying to comfort his new friend. "How about you, Brett?"

"More," responded a cotton-mouthed Brett.

Joe smiled. "Is it OK if I hang with you guys? I don't know anyone else here," he pleaded as a young man with lime hair, a nose ring, bad skin, baggy sagging pants, and a thrift store gold cardigan sweater approached them, slinking.

"You boys look new. I'm Suzanne Boogermaker," he vamped, tastelessly impersonating the character Suzanne Sugarbaker from television's *Designing Women*.

Brett, Damon, and Joe never went to another meeting. They did not need to. They had found each other and became inseparable friends. The following September, they moved into their house, leaving memories of the dorms, and Josh, behind.

• ⤳

At about the same time that Steven returned to Oregon, enrolled in college, and moved to Eugene, a statewide anti-gay initiative campaign began to heat up, heading for a November boil. The media had a field day with this emotional, controversial issue, regularly covering it in newscasts and newspapers and discussing it on talk-radio. Everywhere we looked there were bumper stickers, buttons, and yard signs reminding us of its presence.

Reports of violence against gays, lesbians, bisexuals, transgenders, and their supporters began to surface, exposing the depth of the hate and divisiveness inherent in the issue. The most serious incident occurred in late-September in Salem: A Molotov cocktail–triggered fire burned down the home of a lesbian and gay man who were roommates, killing them.

Measure 9 presented me, a gay teacher, with a great dilemma. Either I could continue limiting the visibility of my homosexuality to the pale pink triangle, fading on my rear bumper, or I could speak out. But my desire to help defeat this measure was, in the end, smothered by the fear that getting involved could jeopardize my job, my career, my livelihood. I also had the intimidating memory that four years earlier Oregon voters had repealed limited protection for gays enacted by the governor, protections that affected me as a school employee.

I chose to play it safe. What support I gave the "No On 9" campaign came in anonymous cover charges to fundraisers or money order contributions signed with bogus names. I didn't even discuss the measure at work. Thus, while the campaign closely touched my life, I felt forced to observe it from a distance.

Steven, Brett, Joe, and Damon, on the other hand, chose to play it risky and get involved in the campaign. Actually, Brett and his housemates chose to play it risky. Steven, still quite cautious, had to be convinced that speaking out and taking part in defeating the hateful messages of the campaign was their only choice.

"How can you even consider not getting involved, Steven?" Damon asked, attempting to convince him to join them. "Especially after the Salem fire. Hell, that could have been us."

"Besides," Brett threatened his boyfriend, "I'll withhold all sexual favors unless you go with us to sign on." That was all the pressure he needed to use. Steven didn't know if Brett was serious or not, but he didn't want to find out.

Together, the quartet went to the Eugene "No On 9" office to volunteer their services during the campaign's final month and to leave four nine-dollar checks. They left the office with "No On 9" buttons on their shirts and a yard sign that they immediately pounded into the front lawn with pride. And a hammer.

• ⟩

Several days later, Steven, entering the campus from the shopping district to the west, heard a loud female voice raving wildly. At first he could not decipher her words, but as he approached, her message became painfully clear.

"Save the children! Stop the perverts! Stop their sins! Save our children from the homosexual agenda! Vote yes on Measure 9!" the woman ranted as she attempted to hand out political propaganda to the indifferent passers-by. Steven caught a glimpse of her as she turned away from him.

I should say something to her, confront her, he thought. But what? I don't know what to say to somebody like that. Besides, I'm late for lit class, his thoughts continued as he looked over his shoulder again, directly at the young woman this time.

Steven stopped.

"Oh, my God. It's Allyson!" he gasped.

Impulsively, he began running toward the girl who had shattered his life years earlier.

"Save the children, my ass, you hypocritical bitch!" Steven raged. "You're a baby killer! You killed my baby! My baby!"

"What?" Allyson asked in a puzzled tone as she turned toward the charging young man, looking first at his face, then noticing his "No On 9" button, and then looking up at his face again. "Oh, Lord. Steven? Steven?"

"Yes, Allyson, it's Steven. You hypocrite. You aborted my baby, and now you're talking about saving the children?"

Allyson stared in shocked disbelief, needing only a moment to recover.

"But I've found Jesus, Steven," her voice smiled.

"The fuck you have, you hypocritical bitch," he screamed, releasing the years of pent-up anger and resentment. Grabbing the pamphlets from Allyson's hand, Steven ordered, "Get the hell out of my face right now! And don't let me ever catch you handing out this shit again or I'll make you wish you never fucked me!"

Allyson went pale, quickly spun around, and stumbled, stunned, through the crowd that had assembled. As she retreated, the crowd, who moments earlier had been aloof and uninvolved, began to cheer spontaneously, surrounding Steven and patting him on his back.

"Where are you going, Allyson?" he called after her. "To your church to join the other liars, other hypocrites, other false Christians?"

Steven exhaled slowly. The demons from his past were finally exorcised. He ignored the congratulatory touches, stepped through the onlookers, held his head upright, and, as if nothing had happened, headed to class. And into the future.

• ⟶

A week later, Steven received a telephone call from the "No On 9" office.

"We need people to go up to Corvallis next Wednesday to support our representatives at a panel discussion of the initiative. All you need to do is be in the audience, ask the right questions, and, maybe, help out if the crowd gets unruly. And that probably won't happen. It'll be at 7:00 p.m. at a middle school near the Oregon State campus. Can you or any of your friends help us?" a businesslike woman named Leslie inquired with a hint of pressure in her voice.

"Wednesday? Yeah, I guess I can, and I'll see if the other guys can go, too," volunteered Steven.

Leslie gave him the address, driving instructions, and some general suggestions for effective audience participation. "I don't know who our two speakers are," Leslie added. "One is an OSU student. That's all I know. I have no idea who the other side is sending. Just be prepared and be careful."

At 6:00 p.m. Wednesday, Steven, hair still damp from his post-run shower, and Brett, just off a four-hour shift at the library, hopped into Steven's spotless pickup. Joe had a paper due the next day and could not go. Damon had a prior commitment, working on a campaign mailing at the "No On 9" office.

As Steven and Brett glided northbound on the two-lane road connecting Eugene and Corvallis, they readied themselves for the uncertainty ahead.

"This could be pretty confrontational," Brett warned. "Are you ready for that?"

"I don't know. I just don't know what to expect. But, remember, our job is to ask questions favorable to our side and to disprove anything their supporters say."

The boys raced the digital clock on the dashboard to Corvallis, nervously looking out the truck's windows. Freshly painted farm houses flew by as some once-red run-down barns next to withered wooden homes seemed to stand still in time along the road.

"We should be there in about half an hour," one of them said as 6:22 glared impatiently at them.

And they did arrive in half an hour, among a sprinkling of cars trickling into the school parking lot.

"There doesn't seem to be much interest in this meeting," Steven observed with disappointment. "Let's just sit here for a few minutes, relax, and watch the people arrive."

"OK," Brett agreed. "But, hey, look at all the people pulling in at that end," he added, pointing. "There must be a huge lot down there. Shit, look at all the people. For a second, I thought this was going to be easy."

"Jesus Christ. Look at them all! We've got to get inside fast and find some seats," Steven said as he opened the truck door and jumped out.

Standing in the doorway at the rear of the auditorium, Brett and Steven scanned the mostly filled chairs.

"There must be three hundred people here. And I'm afraid to find out which side they're on. This is scarier than I thought," Brett whispered through a mouth as dry as an Eastern Oregon summer.

"I see two seats over there," Steven noted, indicating the far end of a near rear row.

The pair quickly skirted the room, seated themselves, and then silently studied the unfamiliar faces around them, eavesdropping on their small talk.

"Who are these people anyway?" Steven asked rhetorically after several moments.

"Why they're typical middle Americans, just like you and me, Homer!" Brett teased.

A pale, pot-bellied gray-haired man wearing a cheap, plaid sports coat climbed the steps leading to the center of the stage at the front of the auditorium.

"Could our panelists, please, come up and seat themselves so we can begin?" he called out, motioning toward the table and five folding chairs to his left.

A middle-aged woman in a black-and-white patterned dress and a hair-style similar to that Rose Marie wore on *The Dick Van Dyke Show* nearly thirty years earlier, stepped up to the stage first, followed by a younger, tall and slender, hard-featured man. "Yes On 9" buttons adorned their lapels. They appropriately sat at the right end of the table, the far right.

From the base of the left side of the stage, an attractive, professional-looking woman of about thirty-five, climbed onto the stage. Then a blond young man with a bi-level haircut and all-American-boy looks ran up the center stage steps to join the woman at the left end of the table.

The man in the sports coat picked up a microphone from the table and began his introductory remarks.

"We are here tonight to discuss Measure 9. We know this is a controversial issue and that many people on each side feel very strongly about it. We urge, therefore, that tonight we all act responsibly and respectfully and keep our emotions in control.

"Representing the 'Yes On 9' campaign are Norma Butkowski, a church secretary, and Ron Stern, a Wilsonville businessman. From 'No On 9' we have Karin Gireaux, a professor of nursing down the road a bit at something called the University of Oregon," he joked, triggering mixed laughter and boos from the OSU-biased audience.

"Joining Karin is a student from right here at OSU, Chad Swanson."

"Chad Swanson" echoed in Steven's ears. He recognized the name. It's Chad! I don't believe it. I don't fucking believe it! he exclaimed to himself in shock. It was the youthful rancher with whom Steven had had his first, awkward sexual experience at the State High School Track Championships several years earlier. Tapping Brett's thigh, Steven excitedly turned to whisper that he knew the blond panelist, and then, realizing that it was better left unsaid, mumbled, "Never mind."

"That blond guy is a nice-looking man, don't you think?" Brett innocently asked as Steven pulled back.

"I guess," Steven responded in an uncommitted tone, "if you like wholesome, handsome guys with shiny smiles, beautiful hair, broad shoulders, and a narrow flat waist."

Ron Stern began the debate with a brief statement in support of the measure. It was full of lies, exaggerations, red herrings, and words, phrases, and images chosen purely to ignite fears, anger, and hate in the audience. Scattered sounds of approval bubbled from the crowd. Karin Gireaux, having taken notes during Stern's orchestrated presentation, then countered every misleading point he made in a calm, organized manner.

Norma Butkowski spoke—no, preached—next, concentrating on the "sin" of homosexuality, frequently referring to Scripture. Never did she actually discuss the words, intent, effects, or specifics of the initiative. Her obsession with male-to-male sex acts and selective use of and biased interpretation of the Bible caused sporadic sniggering in the uncomfortable audience.

Chad, following Mrs. Butkowski, relieved the onlookers' tension by humorously saying, "Wow. That is a weird act to follow. I feel like I'm on the Praise the Lord Network with my favorite 'Christian.' Ma'am, are you sure your name isn't Tammy Faye?"

Most of the audience exploded in cheers, laughter, whistles, and applause. For the first time Steven and Brett sensed support in the air.

"Listen," Chad continued when silence was restored. "I'm not going to make a prepared statement. I'd rather answer your questions. I don't want to talk to you; I want to talk with you about the importance of the decision you will make regarding this sensitive issue on election day."

"OK then," a man wearing a dirty baseball cap boasting a Portland Trailblazer logo yelled from the rear of the room. "Why should we allow perverts to teach our kids, to touch our kids in public schools? Schools, I should add, that we taxpayers pay for."

"Well, I agree, Sir," Chad responded, humoring the man. "We shouldn't allow perverts of any kind to teach or touch . . . "

"God created Adam and Eve, you know, not Adam and Steve," the man interrupted loudly.

"And gay and lesbian people pay taxes, too," Chad said, trying to recapture the flow of his response.

"If God wanted all you perverts here, he wouldn't be killing you all with AIDS," the man continued.

"AIDS is killing all kinds of people, Sir. Have you ever heard of Ryan White? Or Amanda Blake? She played Miss Kitty on *Gunsmoke*. Does anyone here remember *Gunsmoke*?" Many of the grayer heads in the audience nodded. "Well, she died of AIDS. I don't believe either of them were homosexual men," Chad defended calmly. "But this initiative isn't about AIDS. It is about discrimination, dignity, freedom, rights, liberty and all the other ideals our flag stands for and our military . . . "

"Dignity?" the verbal assault continued. "How could someone like you know about dignity? And don't even mention the military. I fought in Vietnam. I didn't do that for no faggots."

From the center of the large hall, a woman's warm voice, worn by a lifetime of gentle reprimands, broke into Mr. Dirty Cap's third interruption. "Wait a minute, Mister!" she blurted as she stood. "You're being rude. Let the young man speak. And I won't tolerate any name-calling!" she added, pointing a firm finger at him. "I came here to learn something tonight, to listen. I'm seventy-one years old, and this is the first time I can remember Corvallis having the guts to talk about homosexuality outside a hypocritical church sermon or school yard joke fest. It's 1992, and it's about time!"

An uncomfortable silence filled the room as the woman sat down.

"Thank you, Ma'am," Chad acknowledged. "I think most of the people here agree with you. Now, I'd like to say something about the military, what I believe its purpose is, and how it relates to Measure 9."

"No. I'd like to do that, Chad, if it's OK?" a man's voice broke in as he waved his hand.

It was Steven.

"Sure," Chad reacted, somewhat befuddled.

"I just completed two years in the U.S. Army," Steven began. "I don't know why the man who interrupted you served in Vietnam. But I'll bet that since he just used the word 'faggot,' he probably used terms like 'gooks' and 'slant eyes' during his tour of duty. And he probably considered some of his own squad to be 'niggers.' But he didn't dare say that word out loud, although he thought it. Well, there's no difference between the words 'nigger,' 'gook,' and 'faggot.' They're all born out of hate, ignorance, and a skewed sense of superiority. Hate, however, is not superior to anything.

"Again, I don't know why he served in Vietnam. But I do know why I served in the army. First and foremost, I served to protect our borders from invasion. And I served to protect the constitutional ideals of freedom, democracy, and the rights of all people anywhere, whether they are in the majority or the minority. I joined the greatest military force in the world to assure minorities everywhere of their safety from the power of hate and persecution that majorities have so often imposed on those they perceive as different or a threat to their control.

"And that is what Measure 9 is about, the fear that if gays, lesbians, and bisexuals are guaranteed equal protection from discrimination and hate, then the control held by the heterosexual majority somehow will be threatened. Measure 9 is not about sexual orientation. It is really about abuse of power and control, and how that can lead to total disregard for the rights of individuals and minority groups. It is about bullying, whether it is done by one person at school or through a majority at the ballot box."

Steven took a deep breath and sat down as a shocked Brett reached over to supportively grab his hand. With a sense of pride and defiance he had never before felt, Steven clasped Brett's hand in his as his insides began to shake violently in a nervous release of years of built-up anger. It was their first public display of affection.

A gentle pat met his left shoulder from the row behind him. A nearby adolescent voice gasped, "That was cool, Mister." And the fizzing sounds of exhaled air, folding-chairs creaking, and whispered reactions enveloped the room.

"God, I'm proud of you, Babe," Brett breathed, smiling at Steven. "Where'd that come from?"

"I don't know. I really don't know! I can't believe I just did that," Steven mumbled in total surprise. "But I had to."

From the stage, Chad ended the auditorium hush. "I couldn't have said that better. Thank you. And thank you for serving our nation."

The discussion continued for nearly forty-five more minutes. Steven heard little of it, though. His attention had shifted to the interested, interesting faces around him. He was fascinated by them, now, and how they seemed to be listening intently to Karin's and Chad's message. Neither he nor many of the others noticed that the man in the dirty cap had silently sneaked, stoop-shouldered, out the rear door of the auditorium.

Immediately upon the meeting's adjournment, Chad leaped from the stage and through the human obstacle course to Steven's side.

"That was terrific. Really!" he opened. "But I have to ask if I know you from campus. You look familiar to me," he rattled on.

"No. I go to U of O," Steven answered. "But, yes, you do know me. You don't remember from where, though, do you, Chad?" he asked as both Chad's and Brett's faces filled with question marks. "You really don't remember?"

"Well, no. I just feel like I've seen you before."

"I'm Steven Shepherd."

"You are? You are!" Chad spurted, lunging toward Steven, embracing him impulsively. "Do you know how often I've thought about you, wondered how you're doing?"

"Am I missing something?" Brett interjected.

"I'll explain it in the truck. Chad, this is my . . . um, lover, Brett," Steven boasted awkwardly, grabbing his familiar hand again. It was the first time Steven had introduced Brett that way.

"This is Brett? The one you told me about?"

"The very same," Steven crowed with pride.

"After all these years? You have got to be kidding!" Chad gasped. "This is so cool. You and him. Wow!" he exclaimed in disbelief. "And you're OK," he added with a sense of relief. "And I'm OK. That's got to be some kind of miracle, 'cuz, Dude, we were both messes back then. Wrecks. Like we were major fucked up."

"Yeah," Steven agreed. "But not as fucked up as that jerk in the dirty Trailblazers cap."

• ⮞

As soon as Steven drove the pickup onto the highway, Brett turned to him and spoke.

"So, who is he?" he asked with more curiosity than suspicion.

"I met him at the state meet in the spring of our senior year," Steven answered without hesitation.

"Well," Brett volleyed bluntly, "did you do him?"

Steven paused, startled by Brett's directness. "Yeah. I did. But it was real weird. It was the first time for either of us. And neither of us knew what we were doing. It was almost funny."

"At least I know you've got good taste!" Brett allowed with a trusting smile.

"I must have totally bored his ears off, though, talking about you," Steven recalled.

A moment passed. Brett leaned over and gently kissed Steven's cheek. "I really love you, Steven. And, damn, was I proud of you tonight."

On election night, two weeks later, while Damon and Joe waited with other volunteers at the "No On 9" office, Steven and Brett watched the returns on the small television in Steven's boarding-house room. Stretched across the rickety, aching, aging bed that also served as their dinner table, they distractedly dined on sausage, olive, and green pepper pizza from Pizza My Heart. A six-pack of Henry's was selected as the Tuesday brew.

Brett wore green U of O Duck gym shorts and an open green and blue flannel shirt. As they finished eating, Steven, wearing only gray army sweat pants, discovered a tomato paste–painted olive next to Brett's right nipple and licked it off.

"Now I'm full," he belched. "There's a big piece left, if you want it." Brett shook his head, his eyes directed on the flickering screen.

"Look, we're ahead!" he blurted as Steven lay the near-empty pizza box on the floor next to the bed.

Two hours and six beers later, the "No" votes, maintaining their lead, appeared to assure a "No On 9" victory.

"Let's call Tim," Steven suggested in semislurred syllables, as he reached for the telephone.

I was heading into the kitchen to toss out my second empty Henry's bottle when the telephone rang. I returned to the living room, turned down my television's volume, and grabbed the phone's receiver.

"Hello. Election Central," I answered, not knowing who the caller was, but anticipating the subject of the call.

"Can you believe this? You are watching the returns, aren't you?" Steven shot back.

"Of course, I am. And yes, this is unbelievable. How are you guys anyway?" I inquired.

"Almost naked. But we wanted to call and share this victory with you before we got completely naked."

"OK, you guys, go do whatever it is you do, but don't ever forget this day. This is really a special moment for all of us, even if things aren't going as well in Colorado. We'll talk later," I suggested, freeing them from the phone.

When Brett and Steven awoke intertwined the next morning, the leftover pizza slice lay dried and cold in its box on the floor next to the bed. A pair of green gym shorts lay on top of it. Gray sweat pants hung precariously from the side of the bed, one inside-out leg clinging desperately around Steven's ankle.

• ⟶

Steven officially moved into the house with Brett, Damon, and Joe between Christmas and New Year's Day, setting up the smallest bedroom as his study. He only slept there when he dozed off at his desk. Brett's bed had become his.

Their relationship flourished. Anger, jealousy, insecurities, petty arguments barely existed. It was as if they cherished every moment they had together, constantly aware of how many moments, years, they had wasted hiding their real feelings. Their love, loyalty, trust, and respect for each other seemed to fend off any challenges to their relationship, and it appeared to be strong and impenetrable.

However, one unexpected challenge to their happiness did occur just weeks into the new year.

One evening, while Steven was studying and Brett worked a late shift at the library, the phone rang, shattering Steven's concentration.

"Man, what I had to go through to find you," an unfamiliar voice teased. "For some reason, I thought your last name was Shafer. The phone book didn't list you. New listings didn't have you. Even the 'No On 9' office couldn't find a Steven Shafer. And then while I was home over Christmas, it dawned on me. Your name is Shepherd, not Shafer. Remember, I am a blond. This is Chad . . . Swanson."

"Well, hi," Steven spurted in surprise. "What's up?"

"I just wanted to tell you again how cool it was seeing you last October and ask you something I've been wondering about ever since. Do you still run?"

"Run? Not competitively. But, yes, I still run," Steven responded.

"Why aren't you competing?" Chad pried. "You were fantastic. You could have made the Olympics."

"Well, basically, it's because I don't want the constant training. I think there are more important things for me to do. Besides, I don't want to be thought of as a runner only. There's more to me than that. Running is something I do; it is not who I am. And I also don't need to run from the things I ran from before. Now I can face them," Steven explained with confidence.

"I can relate to that, Dude. But you really had potential," Chad reflected. "Anyway, as fate would have it, I'll be in Eugene on Saturday for a campaign follow-up meeting. If you're available, maybe we could go for a run together in the morning," Chad proposed.

"Sure. That would be great," Steven said, naively accepting the invitation.

Chad arrived the following Saturday morning just after eight. Silver running tights and a navy blue hooded sweatshirt protected him from the cold Willamette Valley winter.

Steven, in black running shorts, gray U.S. Army sweatshirt, and a green and yellow knit stocking cap, greeted Chad with an innocent hug of friendship and then ran upstairs to kiss Brett, who was still asleep, good-bye. Brett's head was buried under a pillow fortress when Steven peeked into their room. Carefully raising the pillow, Steven lightly pecked his lover's cheek.

"I'll be back in an hour or so. I love you," he whispered as he gently replaced the pillow over Brett's tousled head.

As Steven and Chad hopped down the steps into the front yard where they briefly stretched and warmed up, Steven verbally mapped out the route.

"We start heading east toward I-5, then swing across the river, come back past Autzen Stadium, go into downtown, and cut back across campus," he described.

"Sounds like a good course," Chad said positively.

"Well, of course, it's a good course," quipped Steven.

They trotted together, making small talk, pointing out landmarks and sights along the way. As they neared Autzen Stadium, Chad reached out and pulled at Steven's sleeve near the elbow.

"There's something I've wanted to say to you, tell you. It's awkward, really," he panted, wiping a trickle of sweat sliding down his left temple. "But, you know, when we did it during that meet back when. Well, I was really uncomfortable. Scared," Chad puffed in choppy rhythm. "I didn't know what to do, how to do it. All I knew was that I wanted to do it. I know what I'm doing now. I'd like to have a second chance," Chad propositioned.

Steven, startled by the unforeseen offer, briefly lifted his eyes off the path, looked over at his running partner with a puzzled expression, and stepped crookedly into a slight dent in the dirt. He fell hard, his right knee landing on sharp pebbles on the path, his left palm scraping over a patch of cinders.

"Jesus Christ!" Chad blurted. "Are you OK?"

"Yeah, I'm OK," Steven said, as he turned over on his butt to evaluate the damage. "Nothing major."

"I didn't mean to cause that, Steven," Chad apologized as Steven stared at the path's imprint on his palm. A dribble of blood began to leak from his punctured knee.

"It's all right, Chad. It's not your fault. But I wish you hadn't said that," Steven complained. "You see, I have a lover. I love Brett very much. I loved him even before I met you. I would never hurt him. Not after all we went through."

"This isn't about Brett," rationalized Chad. "I just want to make it up to you. I still think you are a beautiful man."

"What you and I did is a memory, a pleasant memory, Chad, but it is in the past. If you want to be part of my life now, you'll have to be satisfied being a friend. And I would like us to be friends. But those are the terms," Steven spelled out firmly.

"Then we'll be friends," responded Chad, realizing he had no other choice. They looked into each other's eyes for a moment, unsure smiles flickering, and then Chad offered Steven his hand.

"Here. Get up. We gotta complete this course."

"My knee sort of stings. Maybe we should just walk back the short way," Steven suggested, as he took Chad's hand.

"What? Didn't your coach ever tell you about completing the course?" retorted Chad. "You've got to complete the course! The run isn't over because of a minor fall like that. Unless you break an ankle or have a heart attack or something, you gotta complete the course. And even if you do break something, after your ankle heals or your heart mends, you go back and complete the course. That's what running is all about. That's what life is all about, Man."

"OK, but slow down a little. I'm an invalid now," Steven reminded Chad in mock self-pity.

When they returned to the house, completing the course at a pace closer to a fast walk than a slow run, Chad gave Steven a short, careful hug. "Friends," he declared, as he turned and walked to his car.

Steven went inside, showered, and washed and bandaged his wounds. He crawled into the disheveled bed as the awakening Brett reached out to pull him into the warmth of a white linen embrace.

"Did you have a good run, Babe?" Brett mumbled groggily.

"One of the best of my life. I completed the course!"

•⌁

On a late-May afternoon, as Steven prepared for the approaching finals that marked the end of his freshman and his housemates' junior year, Damon Whitaker walked into their sparsely furnished living room carrying a large, battered black case.

"What the hell is this?" he asked, interrupting Steven as he studied. "I found it in the basement," Damon added as he placed it on the table in front of the lumpy, faded sofa where Steven reclined.

"That is my accordion," Steven admitted, looking up. "And now you've found out my deepest, darkest secret," he revealed, bowing his head in false shame. "OK. My name is Steven Shepherd, and I am an accordionist."

"Hi, Steven. Welcome to AA. You are not alone. We've been there, and we can help. But first you must want our help. You can't do this by yourself. We have a twelve-step program to help you overcome this sickness," Damon played along. "Before we can do anything for you, though, you must play something. One final foray into your accordion addiction."

"No way," Steven refused. "I haven't touched that thing in years."

"Please, Steven. I really, really, really love accordion music," Damon whined mockingly, struggling to contain himself.

"Oh, all right, Cry Baby," Steven said, giving in. "But don't expect this to be very good."

"Can accordion music be 'very good'?"

Slipping the straps over his arms, Steven tentatively began drawing a familiar melody from the squeeze box. With each note, his confidence grew and his speed increased to the appropriate cadence. The melody became more recognizable.

"I know that song," Damon shouted. "It's *Mighty Oregon!* Oh, shit, I'm listening to the school fight song on a goddamn accordion. Fuck. I've died and gone to hell!" he groaned.

Urgent footsteps could be heard on the front stairs, the wooden porch, and then in the hall. "Put that thing away," barked Brett, desperately trying to hide his amusement, "or I'll be forced to find my old AC/DC, Def Leppard, and Mötley Crüe cassettes. I love everything about you, Steven Shepherd, but I hate that thing!"

Steven stopped playing. "This number is for the cute guy standing in the back of the room. Come on in. There are empty tables up front. A waitress will be with you in a minute," Steven ad-libbed, looking directly into Brett's brown eyes, as a new tune began escaping from the wheezing instrument.

"You're playing *Point of No Return*," Brett said in disbelief, recognizing the song after several bars. "You're playing Nu Shooz's *Point of No Return!*" he repeated in exaggerated shock, as his eyes locked on Steven's. "On the accordion?" Their eyes remained fastened to each other's as Steven began singing the catchy, repetitive chorus from the Portland group's hit.

"I'm at the point of no return. I'm at the point of no return," he sang over and over as diminuendo faded into silence.

"Hey, Mr. Music Man, want to go upstairs and squeeze my instrument?" Brett invited with a seductive look.

"Spare me the details! I'm out of here," Damon interjected as he ran for the open front door, digging into his tight Levi's pocket for his car keys.

Silently, Brett slid past Steven, stopping on the first step leading upstairs to their bedroom. "Are you coming?" he asked impatiently, looking alluringly over his shoulder.

"Yes, I'm coming, Babe. But first, let me play just one more song," Steven said playfully.

Brett listened a moment. "Why are you playing *Here Comes the Bride?*" he asked curiously.

"It's not called *Here Comes the Bride*," Steven corrected. "It's called *Here Comes the Pride.*"

•➤

A year later, in the spring of 1994, Brett was finishing his undergraduate studies in psychology. His last exam was in a class taught by his favorite professor, a man with whom, over the years, he had shared many after-class discussions and cups of coffee. He confidently sped through the test, completing it faster than most of the other students.

"Well, Exalted Supreme Professor Dude, that's it. That was my final final!" he whispered with a silly smile as he turned in the stapled papers.

"Finally," the professor punned, returning the smile.

"Before I leave, though, I want to thank you for everything you have taught me the past few years," Brett continued, ignoring the play on words.

"That's my job, Brett," the older man replied.

"I'm not talking about in class. I'm talking about as friends," Brett clarified. Then, remembering some unfinished business, he switched tones and topics. "Will I be seeing you in a few weeks?" he asked.

"Of course, you'll see me. I wouldn't miss being there for anything!"

• ⟶

Brett received his bachelor of arts from the University of Oregon several days later, as Steven reached the midpoint in his undergraduate career. But those educational milestones alone were not what etched spring 1994 into their memories. For within weeks of Brett's graduation, in the evening of June 28, in honor of the twenty-fifth anniversary of the Stonewall Rebellion, Steven Matthew Shepherd and Brett Alexander Weiss exchanged vows of love at the Eugene Unitarian Church during a commitment ceremony celebrating their lives together.

I was there. And for the first time in my life, I truly was excited about a wedding.

Steven's parents, Christopher and Josie Shepherd, attended the ceremony, too, having driven from Portland with longtime friends and in-laws to-be, Ray and Jayne Weiss, Brett's parents. But the hour and a half drive to the wedding began with a minor mishap. As Jayne Weiss slid over the sun-baked back seat of the Shepherds' Volvo, she snagged her pantyhose.

"We can stop in Wilsonville to buy a new pair," she suggested. "There's a Fred Meyer right off I-5. It'll only take a sec."

They arrived at the store shortly thereafter and pulled into the vast parking lot as an unexpected narrow strip of rain-filled clouds blew in from the west.

Josie and Jayne ran into the store, aiming for the pantyhose rack, quickly found a flesh-tone pair, and raced it through the shortest check-out line. As they walked back out into the parking lot, a beige station wagon cut them off, impeding their hurried return to their fidgeting, impatient spouses.

"Jayne, look at the bumper sticker on that car," Josie instructed, pointing at the beige wagon. "No Special Rights: Vote Yes On 9" read the weather-worn strip.

Maneuvering hurriedly past the driver's open window, Josie glared at the man's jowly, mustached face and spewed, "You jerk! And I'm not referring to your rude driving, either!" Jayne, embarrassed, grabbed Josie's hand and tugged her toward their waiting car as a misty rain began to fall.

"You won't believe what Josie just did," Jayne shrieked at their husbands, half amused, half angry, as she pushed Mrs. Shepherd into the car. "She just called a guy a jerk."

As the Volvo backed out of its slot, the walrus-faced man walked by. "Hey, you know who that is?" Ray Weiss snapped. "That's the jerk who's pushing all those anti-gay measures. You see him on TV all the time. What's his name?"

"Len Mason," offered Christopher Shepherd.

"Yeah, something like that," agreed Mr. Weiss, as rays of sunlight reappeared through the clouds.

Rainbows arched over their heads as the Shepherds and Weisses escaped the crowded Wilsonville parking lot and turned south on the interstate. The multicolored mirages followed them into the fertile green Willamette Valley, surrounding them like transparent Crayola boxes. In the southern distance, the skies glowed golden gray, leading each of the travelers to believe, silently, that, perhaps, the legendary pot of gold awaited them at the church in Eugene.

"This is very strange, going to the boys' wedding. I mean, who would have ever predicted this?" Jayne asked rhetorically.

Josie responded anyway. "All I know is that they love each other and they're happy. That is all I need to understand."

"Fine. But how can two people who grew up together, who were best friends for so long, become, well, boyfriends? How do I explain that to people?" Christopher Shepherd asked, baring his mixed feelings of approval, self-consciousness, and confusion.

"You don't have to explain it to anyone. You don't have to defend the boys. I don't think they would want that," countered Ray Weiss. "But if you need an answer for yourself, remember that God works in mysterious ways and He doesn't make mistakes. There is a reason they are together. We may not know what it is now, but we do know, as Josie said, that they are happy and have found love. And isn't that all we ever hoped for them? And good health. Maybe their love, their loyalty, is what has kept them healthy. We should be thankful that we're going to watch our sons be married instead of being buried. Too many parents have had to do that."

Steven's and Brett's parents sped through the Willamette Valley in silence, pondering the possibility that God had given their sons an unusual love in order to keep them alive. As the southbound trek continued, the rainbows that had surrounded them at the beginning of their drive evaporated, making way for clear blue skies. But not all the rainbows disappeared. They would find more in the decorations inside the church in Eugene.

The Volvo containing the almost-in-laws arrived at the modest, modern wooden church with more than a half-hour to spare and was greeted by Steven and Brett, who were pacing nervously in front wearing matching traditional tuxedos. After a quick round of kisses, hugs, handshakes, and compliments on clothing, Jayne Weiss went directly into the ladies room to change her pantyhose.

When she emerged, she joined Josie, Christopher, and Ray for a brief explanation of the ceremony given by Damon and Joe, who had organized the entire event. Then, as the guests began to arrive, the boys' parents attempted mingling, clumsily introducing themselves to Steven and Brett's spectrum of friends. The Shepherds greeted their daughter, Crystal, as she stepped into the church foyer, followed by her boyfriend, Craig, cousin Molly from Pendleton, and Lynne Burgess, with whom she had reconciled at Steven's insistence.

"They've got a lot of heterosexual couples for friends," Ray noted to Christopher as they looked around the gathering crowd, focusing on the few pairs that might have fit that description. "I just assumed all their friends would be gay."

"Josie," Jayne whispered in contrast, "have you noticed that the best-looking men here are with other men? I haven't seen as many handsome guys since I looked at *Playgirl*."

"That's for sure," Josie agreed, realizing a moment too late what she had just admitted.

•➤

Just before the ceremony was to begin, as the last of the guests found seats in the sanctuary, Brett approached me nervously, nudging my elbow. "Come over here with me," he requested, leading me to a far corner of the lobby as the remainder of the wedding party clustered by the front door.

"I've never actually thanked you for being there for Steven back at Columbia," Brett began. "You helped him a lot, more than I think you realize. But, more important, I want to thank you for being there for . . . me." He paused, inhaling slowly, deeply. His eyes darted from mine to the Windsor knot topping my striped tie. "I've saved something for you," he continued, "something I have held on to for a long, long time, something I've kept for just the right moment. I only wish . . . ," his words began to drown in his throat, "I had . . . "

Frustrated by his lack of composure, Brett sharply jabbed his hand into his right tuxedo pocket. "Here," he said, barely audible, as he handed me a paper pink triangle, worn and flimsy with age.

My eyes leaped from the gift to Brett's moist eyes. I impulsively hugged him in surprised, relieved silence. It was a long hug. It was also long overdue. When he tried to speak again, I put my right index finger to his lips.

"Shhh, you don't need to say anything. I understand," I said soothingly. "Now, we've got a wedding to start," I reminded him, trying to shake the emotion from my face.

"Hey, everyone," I called across the lobby as I turned to face Steven, the Shepherds, the Weisses, Damon, and Joe, "shouldn't we be in there, too?" As the group moved into the sanctuary, Steven knowingly nodded in my direction. How long the boys had kept this secret, I don't know. But I was extremely glad they had waited until this moment to share it with me. It was the perfect time to answer the last question that lingered in my mind from our days together at Columbia High School.

Moments later, when the minister, Jeffrey Robertson, a slightly built African-American with a high hairline, asked, "Who gives away this groom?" indicating Brett, Mr. Weiss rose and said, "His mother and I do." The church simmered with hushed laughter.

When Reverend Robertson asked, "Who gives away the other groom?" I stood tall and announced, "His parents and I proudly do." Then I sat down next to the beaming parents of "the other groom."

• ⟶

It was a short ceremony, lasting no more than fifteen minutes. But it was unlike any marriage rite ever seen before by its witnesses.

Reverend Robertson spoke briefly of the commitment involved in marriage, the importance of communication, trust, and loyalty.

"But I'm not sure I have to remind you two gentlemen about those things. After all, if I understand this correctly, you've shared a love since kindergarten. That is unusual. Now, granted several years ago you experienced a communication breakdown that had a strong negative effect on your trust, loyalty, and understanding. But anyone who has seen you two together, watched you two, as I have, can see how well you learned the lessons of your youth. Rarely have I seen two individuals who so totally appreciate, respect, and love the other. Therefore, I bless this marriage without reservation, as I am certain, does the Lord," Reverend Robertson said, sanctifying Steven and Brett's union.

When he finished, Brett turned to face his partner.

"I loved you then," he began. "I love you now. I will love you tomorrow. I will love you forever. With you, life has always been like the playground at which we first met. It has always been fun," he told Steven with a playful yet serious smile on his face. "But I never felt that our friendship, our relationship, and later our love, was a game." He reached into his trouser pocket, pulled out a simple gold band and slid it onto the third finger of Steven's right hand. "However, Steven Shepherd, even though I love you more than words, this ring, or a ceremony can express, I must say right now . . . tag, you're it!"

The laughter that emerged from the witnessing friends and relatives was mixed with gentle sniffling and not-so-gentle nose blowing, for no one there had ever heard a wedding vow quite so touching or unique. Brett then lovingly touched the side of Steven's head, caressing it.

Steven, amused and moved, accepted the tag, cleared his throat, took a deep breath, and placed an identical gold band, which he had been clasping in his clammy hand throughout the ceremony, on the third finger of Brett's right hand. He, however, said nothing.

Instead, Steven chose to sing to his partner a medley of songs made famous by Brett's favorite entertainer, Bette Midler. Having grown up in Portland, the Rose City, the boys long ago had learned the melody of its unofficial theme song, *The Rose*. Nevertheless, it came as a total surprise to Brett when Steven began to sing its lyrics a cappella to him. It was not, however, until Steven added the words to *The Wind Beneath My Wings* that Brett, obviously moved, lost control of his upper lip.

My lip quivered, too, as did many around me. But Steven's voice did not quiver. Confidently, proudly, he sang his song of love to Brett, allowing me to hear his baritone tones for the first time. Like everything else he attempted, he did this well, too.

What a truly remarkable guy he is, I thought, recalling feelings I had had years earlier after reading the *Chronicle* interview that had enumerated Steven's many activities and various accomplishments. He sang in the church youth choir, I reminded myself.

After he finished, Steven gently brushed the tears from Brett's cheeks and took him in his arms. Then, before Reverend Robertson had the chance to give his verbal cue, Steven passionately kissed Brett's lips.

"Hey, I'm supposed to say 'You may now kiss each other!'" the minister reprimanded in a futile effort to regain control of the service. "Oh, never mind. I think we're done now," he conceded, smiling, as he reached to encircle both men around the shoulders with his out-stretched arms.

As the pews emptied and the elated people passed into the foyer, Steven rushed to hug his parents and sister, as Brett and his mother and father shared a gigantic three-way embrace.

Then, as if there had been a silent signal, they separated from their families and stepped toward me, together. The contented expressions on their faces cannot be described. We reached for each other, pulling our three bodies together as one. The emotional messages expressed in that hug were unlike any I had ever given or received before. My happiness at that moment dwarfed any joy or ecstasy I had ever experienced, and I celebrated what I perceived to be the completeness, the total fulfillment of my life.

•➜

The wedding party meandered down the aisle through the well-wishers like bumper cars, going nowhere and everywhere at the same time. Eventually, they reached the lobby. It gradually filled with joyful family and friends, who nearly smothered Steven and Brett with a blanket of congratulating hands and smiling faces.

I stepped through the crowd, toward a table supporting a silver coffee urn, a punch bowl brimming with lime-colored froth, and a lonely crystal dish of pastel-painted mints.

A handsome young man with moussed blond hair and a goatee ladled cups of green foam, setting them around the punch bowl.

"Coffee or punch?" he offered as I approached.

"Coffee, please," I opted as the smiling server twisted the urn's knob measuring my dosage of caffeine.

Then he turned to the raven-haired man next to him. "Babe, do you think I should tell Mrs. Shepherd that I was Steven's first homosexual experience?" he asked devilishly.

"No, Chad, I don't think so!" his partner said, adamantly rejecting the facetious suggestion. "She seems awfully cool for a mom. But not that cool."

I rotated toward the crowd, cup in hand, and looked for an empty spot where I could sip my coffee. The wall next to the men's room was vacant, except for a man who stood fidgeting with a set of tinkling keys. He smiled slightly, nervously, as I approached. The man was fortyish, fit, attractive, and vaguely familiar. I stepped to the wall, near him.

"A safe place to drink my coffee," I explained, trying to open the conversation. "No elbows here."

"Tim Lerner?" he asked cautiously, peering into my eyes.

"Yes," I responded, surprised that he knew my name.

"You don't know how long I've been looking for you. And now that I've found you, I don't know what to do. I don't even know what to say. But I've got to say something."

"Say something about what?" I questioned, confused, as he continued looking into my eyes.

"I've rehearsed this in my mind so many times," he continued. "And now that you're here, I don't know how to say it. God, this is hard. I want you to know that I'm sorry," he blurted out. "There, I said it, as if that could make any difference."

"Sorry? For what? I don't understand. Do I know you?" I asked, hoping his name would explain his strange, strained apology.

"No. You don't. Not exactly. I was one of Brett's professors at school. But that isn't why you should know me. My name is John Christianson."

The name stunned me like a blind-side quarterback sack. I fell against the wall, spilling some suddenly unimportant coffee on the floor.

"You're kidding?" I asked, knowing that he wasn't. My heart began beating, pounding, racing like an approaching train. I could feel it in my stomach, throat, and forehead. I could even feel it in my teeth.

"No. Regretfully, I'm not. I take it, you know who I am, then?" he assumed with a sadness in his voice that sounded as if it had been there for years.

"Yes. I know who you are."

"Listen, is this really uncomfortable for you? Of course, it is. What am I asking for? I just want you to know that I'm sorry. I've been sorry since the day it happened. Remember? I apologized then. Please, understand that," he begged as his voice cracked. "Can we go outside, where we can be alone, and talk? Besides, I really have to have a smoke!" he said, pulling a pack of Camels from his pocket as he led me through the door.

We stepped out of the church and into the fading colors of late June dusk. John shakily lit a cigarette, his hands trembling as violently as my heart pounded.

"Tim. Tell me you're OK. Just tell me that. Are you OK?" he pleaded as soon as smoke began rising from his fingers.

"Yeah, I'm OK," I muttered, surprised by the unexpected confrontation, overwhelmed by his apparent remorse, and confused by my own feelings.

"God, I needed to know that, even if you hate my guts."

"I don't hate your guts, John," I told him, although he did not stop talking long enough to hear me.

"You have every right to. I understand that. But I just want you to know, Tim, that I did not want that to happen to you. I did not want to do it. I just didn't know how to stop him. He was a maniac," he rattled on.

"John, first of all, please, relax," I said, attempting to calm him. I waited a moment before I went on, allowing him a much-needed long, deep drag from his cigarette. "I don't hate you. I never hated you. You were nice to me. Remember? I couldn't understand that. Why were you nice to me? Why were you even there? I know why I was there. I know why he was there. But I don't know why you were there. Tell me. I've only waited twenty-five years to find out why that nightmare happened to me. Help me, John. Help me make some sense of it. Please," I appealed, taking my turn at pleading.

"About a year before you got . . . " he began, pausing unsuccessfully to search for a less painful word, "raped, he raped me. You see, I sort of hung out with him and his friends. I was a fifth wheel, though, a hanger-on, a wannabe, although we didn't have that word then. The other guys didn't particularly like me, and I knew it. But he seemed to, and he was the leader, so they let me run around with them They were cool guys, jocks, football players. I wasn't. They had cars. I didn't. So I did whatever I had to do to be part of the crowd, never dreaming that it would include being raped by that madman," John rattled at a rat-a-tat pace, never mentioning Rick German's name.

"One night when we were alone, and I think he planned it that way, he got me drunk. Very drunk. And that's when he did it. He was not drunk, though. He never got drunk for sex. It was like he wanted to be perfectly aware of the torture he put others through. He invited me over to his house while his folks were gone. We were in his room sort of wrestling around when he grabbed my arm and threatened to break it if I didn't drop my pants. He was serious. I had no choice. It was a lot like what happened to you, only we were facing a mirror and I could see the evil in his eyes. It didn't take him very long; it never did. When he was done, he called me a queer and threw me out of his house. I left, in pain, shocked, traumatized beyond tears. He called me the next day and warned me that if I ever told anyone or refused him in the future, he would tell everyone that I was a queer, that I had tried to get him to fuck me, that I enjoyed getting fucked.

"Well, the irony was that I was a queer. I was just beginning to understand that. But I certainly wasn't going to let anyone else know. After all, it was before Stonewall. So I became his sex-slave to protect myself and my reputation. Then I realized that even if I were able to avoid him or refuse him, he'd just go and rape somebody else and bribe them into sex-slavery, too. After totally ruining my life with his lies, of course. So, I was put in the position of having sex with him to protect other people as well as myself. Or, so I thought.

"The next summer, the summer he got you, he became obsessed with 'the campus can' and terrorizing queers there, never admitting that he was one himself. And he would make me participate by threatening me. You weren't the first one we got, Tim. The first one was an older man who cried through the whole thing. He had a wedding ring on. The second was a drunk guy who actually seemed to enjoy it. That pissed the asshole off so bad that he couldn't get it up. So he demanded we go back the next night. That's when you came along.

"We saw you arrive at the top of the hill on your bike. I immediately recognized you from school. I prayed you'd go away before it got darker. But you didn't. You were so young, Tim. You were so goddamn young. And innocent," John raced through his recounting of that night, finally taking a breath.

"And beautiful. I tried to stop him right there in our hideaway in the bushes. I tried stroking his crotch. I even offered my butt, bumping it up against him. But he wasn't interested in me anymore. He wanted you. He wanted a new victim.

"Eventually, you began to ride down the slope to your inevitable torture, and I gambled on an idea I had. 'Can I fuck him when you're done?' I asked. 'I suppose,' he allowed begrudgingly. 'You can have sloppy seconds. But that's this time only. Remember, you take it, you little faggot. You don't give it.' I don't know why he agreed. But he did. And that's how I got time with you. I had to have time with you because I knew how you would feel when it was over. I knew that you would need someone to hold you, to calm you. I could feel his adrenaline pumping as you neared that damn place. 'Nice ass on that little faggot. And it's mine,' I heard him faintly breathe as he watched you park your bike. You were nothing more to him than another nameless, faceless faggot.

"But you weren't faceless to me. I knew who you were. You were . . . oh, God, this is embarrassing after all these years . . . that sophomore with the magnetic eyes who passed my locker every day, on your way to Lindstrom's world history class, never noticing that I would turn and watch you as soon as you passed. I even knew your name, although I didn't know you. But I wanted to know you. Yes, I had wanted to know you. Only not there, not at 'the campus can.'"

John's voice finally trailed off, like an old record turned off in midgroove. He silently stared straight ahead, unfocused, while I gazed, speechless, at my shoes, trying to absorb all that I had just heard.

"I tried to stop him, Tim. I really tried," he whispered in an emotionally exhausted voice. He turned to face me as I looked up. Our eyes met. "I've thought about you a million times since then," he declared in a slightly stronger tone. "I've wondered if you just stumbled into 'the campus can' by accident that night or if you had gone there intentionally. I've wondered if he affected your life as negatively as he had mine. I've wondered if suicide or AIDS had taken you to your grave . . . before I could find you, before I had the chance to apologize. I wondered why I couldn't find you in Seattle when I returned from Nam," he continued rambling, purging himself of more twenty-five-year-old pain.

"What happened to Rick in Nam?" I interrupted with curiosity, remembering the alleged reports of "friendly fire."

"Oh, you know who he was, then. You know about Nam." His tone changed, becoming deadly serious. "I don't want to talk about that. Ever," John stated flatly.

"OK," I obeyed, understanding totally. "Didn't they call you J.C. in school?" I asked, trying to steer the conversation toward less sensitive subjects.

"Yeah," he responded unenthusiastically.

"J.C., like in Jesus Christ?" I insensitively reminded him again.

"I'm John now."

"Well, John, let me tell you about my search for a guy named J.C. and how after all these years I find him at, of all places, a church. But let me tell you about that at dinner. You see, I've got these 'magnetic' eyes, and they'd really love to look at you across a candle-lit table. They've been wanting to look at you for a quarter of a century."

For the first time since we began talking, John Christianson smiled. It was a stiff smile, initially rusty, unpracticed. It seemed to struggle, trying to loosen itself from past restraints. I reached out and took his hand. His smile broke free, shedding warm light across his face and onto my heart. "Smiling has always been difficult for me," he said self-consciously. "Never had much reason to smile. Until now." Then he reached out to me, gently cupped my shoulders in his hands and pulled me into a long, healing, desperately needed embrace, as Steven and Brett watched, hand-in-hand, through a crystal-clear church window.

I realized that John's touch had not changed in twenty-five years.

•╼

EPILOGUE

I slept with John for the first time a week later. It was the Fourth of July, the day Americans celebrate freedom, all kinds of freedom. Political freedom. Personal freedom. Freedom from the past.

Fireworks danced in the skies of America that night. We watched Portland's display explode over the Willamette River from the deck of my West Hills condo and then we went to bed. An entirely different kind of fireworks took place there. We fell asleep immediately afterward, saying nothing to each other, nothing verbally that is, and as we slept on our sides, nestled like spoons in a silverware tray, a satisfied smile curled my lips.

I was dreaming.

It was that dream again, the one that had haunted me for years, the one in which an alluring neon invitation illuminated a deserted section of sidewalk. I was lying, as I always did in this dream, on my back on the concrete. A man with shoulder-length hair knelt between my legs. Only this time, the man finally had a face. It was John.

As I dreamt, John, too, was dreaming.

In his dream, he was waiting, crouched in a Vietnamese jungle, just out of earshot of his unit's makeshift camp, allegedly scouting the area for enemy. Suddenly, a knot of tropical vines parted. As John had hoped, Rick German, grime and sweat covering his face and staining his camouflage clothing, stepped through the vines toward him, not suspecting that considerable time had been spent tracking him down, setting him up.

"Hey, Jayce," German blurted out with surprise. "I heard you were nearby. I been lookin' for you," he added, as aircraft noises hovered in the distance. "Hell, look at you. You're still a little pansy! Even with that." He demeaned John one final time, pointing to the gun-metal gray M-16 in John's hand.

Without deliberation, without allowing Rick German time to react, John lifted the military rifle, aimed it, and blasted German directly in the heart, splattering him all over the strangling foliage around them.

"There," John exhaled in relief. "Now you really don't have a heart."

At precisely the same moment that Rick German's "mysterious" death replayed for the final time in John Christianson's dreams, a single store-bought firework, perhaps a cherry-bomb, erupted in a nearby West Portland yard. John's eyes opened with an explosive start and stared at his unfamiliar surroundings for a moment. Then, recognizing them, John Christianson relaxed. It was the first time since his life had been shattered in that stifling bedroom decades earlier that he had relaxed, totally relaxed. He firmly but gently grabbed my hand. Faintly, in the back of his mind, in the furthest corner of his memory, John could hear Mick Jagger sing It's All Over Now.

"Yeah," a contented John mumbled, just loud enough for me to hear in my post-dream semiconsciousness. "Now." And he calmly closed his eyes, his lips slipping into a smile that reflected the long-awaited satisfaction of completing the course.

•‿